M. TULLI CICERONIS

PRO ARCHIA POETA

ORATIO

CICERO

PRO ARCHIA POETA ORATIO

A STRUCTURAL ANALYSIS OF THE SPEECH
AND
COMPANION TO THE COMMENTARY

STEVEN M. CERUTTI

BOLCHAZY-CARDUCCI PUBLISHERS, INC.
WAUCONDA, ILLINOIS

General Editor
Laurie K. Haight

Contributing Editors
Aaron Baker
Allan Kershaw

Cover Illustration
This denarius, minted in Rome ca. 66 B.C. by Q. Pomponius Musa,
is one of a series of nine types, each depicting on its reverse
one of the nine muses. Shown here is Calliope, the Muse of epic poetry,
playing the lyre while resting it on a column.
(Photograph courtesy of the American Numismatic Society)

Cover Design
Charlene M. Hernandez

Bolchazy-Carducci Publishers, Inc.
1000 Brown Street, Unit 101
Wauconda, Illinois 60084 USA

http://www.bolchazy.com

ISBN 0-86516-439-8

Printed in the United States of America
1999
by Trade Service Publications

Library of Congress Cataloging-in-Publication Data

Cicero, Marcus Tullius.
    [Pro archia. English & Latin]
    Pro archia poeta oratio / Cicero ; a structural analysis of the
speech and companion to the commentary, Steven M. Cerutti.
      p.   cm.
    ISBN 0-86516-439-8 (pbk. : alk. paper)
    1. Speeches, addresses, etc., Latin—Translations into English.
2. Speeches, addresses, etc., Latin—History and criticism. 3.
Cicero, Marcus Tullius. Pro Archia. 4. Cicero, Marcus
Tullius—Technique. 5. Rhetoric, Ancient. 6. Oratory, Ancient. I.
Cerutti, Steven M. II. Title.
PA6307 .A9 1999
875'.01–dc21
                                     99-21314
                                      CIP

For my Mother and Father

Quis est nostrum liberaliter educatus cui non educatores, cui non magistri sui atque doctores, cui non locus ipse ille mutus ubi alitus aut doctus est cum grata recordatione in mente versetur? Cuius opes tantae esse possunt aut umquam fuerunt quae sine multorum amicorum officiis stare possint? Quae certe sublata memoria et gratia nulla exstare possunt.

— Marcus Tullius Cicero
Pro Plancio (81.10–16)

CONTENTS

PREFACE

———◆———

 The structural analysis of Cicero's *Pro Archia* offered in the pages that follow has been more than a decade in generation. It began during the summer of 1985 when, as an undergraduate at the University of Iowa, I first worked through Harold Gotoff's excellent stylistic commentary, *Cicero's Elegant Style: An Analysis of the Pro Archia* (Urbana: University of Illinois Press, 1979), as part of an extra-curricular reading group organized by Joseph Hughes, then a graduate student, today a Professor of Classics at Southwest Missouri State University. The influence that both of these exceptional Latinists have had on my own career as a classicist has been profound, and will no doubt show on every page of this work. What will also show, I hope, is my deep appreciation for Cicero's Latin artistry, however shallow my understanding still may be.

 Since first reading the *Pro Archia*, I have had the pleasure of teaching the speech many times to students at both the undergraduate and graduate level. Over the years I have tried a number of different commentaries, but found none that combined both a stylistic treatment of the speech with a thorough complement of grammatical notes. In 1998 I published the first installment of a two volume edition of and commentary on the *Pro Archia* that I hoped would meet this need. The present volume, containing detailed diagrams of nearly every the oration, is offered as the second installment to serve as a companion to the first volume.

For the past three years I have enjoyed the leisure of being able to spend many of my days teaching Cicero's *Pro Archia*, and most of my nights writing about it. Therefore, it is safe to say that both volumes have been validated by every student who passed through my upper-level Latin classes, as each contributed to, as well as profited from, my efforts. And while it would certainly be implausible to mention each student by name here, it would be impossible not to acknowledge three key individuals who have helped make this second volume a reality.

For their vigilant attention to every particular of the diagrams contained in the pages that follow, I am indebted to Aaron Baker and Allan Kershaw, fine Latinists both, who delivered me from many macroscopic errors in a work fraught with microscopic detail. Finally, I must thank Laurie Haight, my principle editor at Bolchazy-Carducci, an accomplished Latinist in her own right, whose circumspect oversight of every aspect of the publishing process brought this book to press.

Steven M. Cerutti
East Carolina University
Greenville, North Carolina
St. Valentine's Day, 1999

INTRODUCTION

As the title indicates, this book was designed to be a companion to my 1998 text of and commentary on Cicero's *Pro Archia Poeta Oratio*. But it is also a complete work in its own right, containing comprehensive diagrams and detailed discussions of nearly every sentence of the speech: a sentence-by-sentence structural analysis offered as an aid for anyone undertaking for the first time the challenge of translating Cicero's *Pro Archia*, an oration that has since antiquity been considered one of the finest achievements of Latin literature.

Each diagram provides a sort of roadmap to guide the student through the periodic structure of the Ciceronian sentence, which often seems—especially to the beginner—an impenetrable labyrinth of syntax. I hope the diagrams that follow will not only assist in the process of translation, but will also leave the student with a better understanding of, and deeper appreciation for, the architecture of formal Latin prose.

While the method used in creating the diagrams follows that of no one particular system, it is based, for the most part, on the traditional rules and attendant terminology of Latin grammar and syntax recognized by grammarians for centuries—not to mention the experience of some years in the classroom (both as student and teacher) on the part of the author. But because the proliferation of Latin textbooks on the market today has led to a variety of ways in which even the most standard grammatical concepts are presented, a brief outline of the terms and principles necessary to understand and use the diagrams in this book is given below.

READING THE DIAGRAMS

It is the premise of this book that every Latin sentence, simple or complex, can be broken down into "kernels" and "modifiers." The term "kernel" is used to describe any clause, either main or dependent, stripped of all modifiers and therefore containing only its essential "kernel items" (i.e., subject, verb, and, if there is one, direct object). Each diagram begins with the kernel of the main clause, to which are added, on lines descending from each word, the modifiers of its various kernel items.

In a simple Latin sentence, nouns can be modified by adjectives (which agree with their nouns in case, number, and gender) and by other nouns (only in the genitive case, or in the same case by APPOSITION). A verb can be modified by a single adverb, by a noun in the ablative (means, manner, etc.) or dative (indirect object, agent, etc.) case, or by a prepositional phrase.

Given below is a template for how the kernel of a simple sentence is diagrammed according to the method of this book:

Subject	Verb	Object
adjective	adverb	adjective
noun (gen.)	noun (abl. or dat.)	noun (gen.)
	prepositional phrase	

The diagram of a complex sentence is merely an expansion of the elements found in a simple sentence: entire clauses can substitute for either the subject or direct object of a kernel, or can also function as adjectival or adverbial modifiers. Such clauses are traditionally called dependent or subordinate clauses and are of three kinds:

♦ THE NOUN CLAUSE: this takes the place of the subject or direct object of any kernel, and includes many relative clauses and various accusative + infinitive constructions (i.e., the subject clause of certain verbal constructions, or the indirect statement of a verb with the semantic feature of "thinking," "saying," "seeing," etc.).

♦ THE ADJECTIVAL CLAUSE: this takes the place of a single adjective and includes any relative clause that does not function as a noun clause (i.e., as a kernel item). Included in this category can also be all participial clauses, except the ablative absolute (for which, see below).

♦ THE ADVERBIAL CLAUSE: this modifies the verb of a kernel, is usually introduced by a subordinating conjunction (e.g., *cum*, *quod*, *ut*, *si*, etc.), and expresses such semantic features as purpose, result, etc. In this group should also be included the ablative absolute.

The following English sentence will serve as an example of how a complex sentence is diagrammed according to the guidelines given above:

The big man who leapt nimbly over the wall always sends expensive flowers to his mother because he truly loves her.

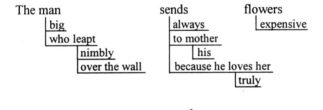

SAMPLE DIAGRAMS

The following two sentences from the *Pro Archia* will provide a step-by-step illustration of how the diagrams in this book are constructed.

Consider the following sentence:

Etenim omnes artes quae ad humanitatem pertinent habent quoddam commune vinculum et quasi cognatione quadam inter se continentur.

The first step is to identify the kernel of the main clause of the sentence. Although it is common for the kernel items of the main clause to be spread out over the span of the entire sentence, often separated from one another by many words, dependent clauses, etc., when the kernel is presented in a diagram, its kernel items are isolated on a single line and arranged in the order in which they appear in the sentence.

Every diagram begins with the isolation of the main kernel:

artes habent vinculum et continentur

Once the kernel items of the main clause are identified, their modifiers can be added. The first, *omnes*, modifies *artes* and therefore appears on the diagram directly under that noun:

artes habent vinculum et continentur
⌊omnes

The next modifier is the adjectival relative clause *quae ad humanitatem pertinent*, the kernel of which is simply *quae pertinent* (the prepositional phrase *ad humanitatem* will be treated separately in the next step). Because its antecedent is also *artes*, *quae...pertinent* appears under *omnes* and is attached to the same line:

artes habent vinculum et continentur
⌊omnes
⌊quae pertinent

Contained within the relative clause, bracketed between its subject (*quae*) and verb (*pertinent*), is the prepositional phrase *ad humanitatem* which, because it modifies *pertinent*, appears under that verb:

artes habent vinculum et continentur
⌊omnes
⌊quae pertinent
          ⌊ad humanitatem

The next two modifiers, *quoddam* and *commune*, both modify *vinculum*, and therefore appear on the diagram under it (note: in order to accommodate all of the modifiers below the words they modify, it often becomes necessary to adjust the spacing between kernel items):

```
artes        habent      vinculum et continentur
 | omnes                   | quoddam
 | quae pertinent          | commune
          | ad humanitatem
```

The next modifier in the sentence is the adverb *quasi*, but because it modifies the ablative *cognatione*, which in turn modifies *continentur*, we must attribute *cognatione* first, and then add *quasi* to it, along with *quadam*, which also modifies *cognatione*:

```
artes        habent      vinculum   et   continentur
 | omnes                  | quoddam       | cognatione
 | quae pertinent         | commune          | quasi
          | ad humanitatem                   | quadam
```

The prepositional phrase *inter se*, an adverbial modifier (as is generally the case for most prepositional phrases in Latin) is also added under *continentur* on the same line as *cognatione*:

```
artes        habent      vinculum   et   continentur
 | omnes                  | quoddam       | cognatione
 | quae pertinent         | commune          | quasi
          | ad humanitatem                   | quadam
                                          | inter se
```

The same basic principles that apply to a relatively simple sentence, such as the one treated above, also obtain when diagramming sentences that are more complex. Take, for example, the following conditional sentence:

Quod si mihi a vobis tribui concedique sentiam, perficiam profecto ut hunc A. Licinium non modo non segregandum, cum sit civis, a numero civium verum etiam, si non esset, putetis asciscendum fuisse.

Although the main kernel of a conditional sentence is, strictly speaking, that of the APODOSIS, with the PROTASIS being an adverbial clause explaining the circumstance(s) or condition(s) attendant upon the action of the verb of the main clause, for the purposes of this study the kernels of both PROTASIS and APODOSIS are presented as parallel independent clauses in the diagram. Furthermore, because Cicero generally constructs conditional sentences with PROTASIS preceding APODOSIS, conditions are always diagrammed in this order:

PROTASIS:

Quod si tribui concedique sentiam

APODOSIS:

perficiam

Once the kernels of the PROTASIS and APODOSIS are identified, the modifiers can be added. We begin with those of the PROTASIS: the first is the dative *mihi* which, because it is the indirect object of both *tribui* and *concedi*, is shown by a line that descends from the space between the two words:

PROTASIS:

Quod si tribui concedique sentiam
      ⌊mihi

Likewise, because the prepositional phrase *a vobis*, which shows agency, also modifies both passive infinitives, it appears on the diagram on the same line under *mihi*:

PROTASIS:

Quod si tribui concedique sentiam
      ⌊mihi
      ⌊a vobis

With the diagram of the PROTASIS complete, we now move to the APODOSIS, the kernel of which consists entirely of the verb *perficiam*, modified by the adverb *profecto* and a result clause introduced by *ut*:

APODOSIS:

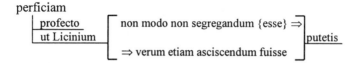

The verb of the *ut* clause (*putetis*) governs two accusative + infinitive indirect statements, arranged in formal symmetry by *non modo...verum etiam*. The kernel items of the clause are presented in such a way as to preserve their word order in the original sentence, with the gerundive verbs of both indirect statements bracketed by the accusative subject (*Licinium*) and governing verb (*putetis*) that they share.

With the kernel items of the *ut* clause now on the diagram, we can add their modifiers, the first of which is the demonstrative pronoun *hunc*, which modifies *Licinium*:

APODOSIS:

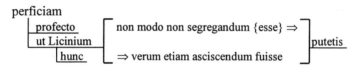

The next two modifiers are a *cum* clause followed by the prepositional phrase *a numero*, both of which modify the verb *non segregandum {esse}*, and so appear under it on the same line:

APODOSIS:

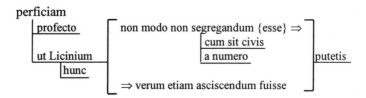

The final modifier of the *non modo* component of the indirect statement is the genitive *civium*, which modifies *numero*:

APODOSIS:

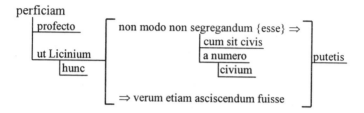

The diagram ends with a the addition of the adverbial *si* clause modifying *asciscendum fuisse*:

APODOSIS:

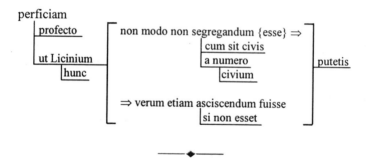

USING THIS BOOK

Users of this book will discover, as they work through the diagrams, that certain sentences have been omitted from this study. The decision to omit one sentence and include another was based on an evaluation of the rhetorical complexity of each sentence, resulting in the exclusion of a small number of the shorter, simpler sentences of the oration in order to allow the student to focus on those sentences whose complex, rhetorical structure merit closer examination.

The guiding principles behind the composition of this book were simplicity and ease of use. Therefore, in order to streamline the diagrams and not complicate them with certain words that have no bearing on kernel items and their modifiers, particles such as *autem*, *enim*, *itaque*, *vero*, etc., have been for the most part omitted. Furthermore, the Latin text of each sentence is accompanied by its diagram underneath it on the same page, with a corresponding translation on the facing page followed by a brief structural analysis, and, where needed, notes explaining any irregular syntactic features. The purpose of including a translation was not to supply a polished final English version of the speech, but rather to provide users of this book with a literal translation that follows the original Latin word order and sentence structure as closely as possible.

Because this book was designed primarily to be used in conjunction with my 1998 commentary on Cicero's *Pro Archia*, the following conventions of that edition have been followed: whenever a rhetorical device is mentioned, it appears in small capitals (e.g., CHIASMUS APODOSIS, etc.), indicating that its definition can be found in Appendix II of that edition. But in order to allow this book to be used independent of the commentary, a copy of that appendix is also supplied at the end of this volume. Furthermore, although all the diagrams (as well as their accompanying notes and translations) have been numbered consecutively, so that both instructor and student can refer to them without having to cite the paragraph and line numbers of the Latin text of my edition, these numerical references are also given at the beginning of the notes for each sentence.

Finally, while symbols in the diagrams have been kept to a minimum, the following few should be noted:

♦ Whenever possible, kernels of compound clauses are presented on a single line. Where space on the page does not allow this, compound kernels are split and presented on separate lines with arrows (⇒) indicating the continuation of the clause.

♦ Because Latin syntax often requires the reader to supply words from one clause to another, whenever it becomes necessary to supply words shared among one or more clauses in a diagram, they appear enclosed within braces ({ }). This applies even when the words supplied must be understood in a different case (as with nouns, adjectives, etc.) or tense (as with verbs) than the form in which they originally appeared in the sentence.

♦ Because Latin verbs are inflected, subject pronouns are often omitted from the kernel. Whenever these are supplied in a diagram, they appear in *italics* and enclosed within brackets ([ ]).

♦ Whenever a line from one section of a diagram overlaps that of another, a broken line (- - - - -) is used instead of the usual solid one in order to avoid confusion.

——————◆——————

A FINAL WORD

Diagramming is an excellent exercise for the student at every level, in that it requires one to account for the syntax of each word or clause in a sentence. Regardless of how much previous experience, if any, students may have had with diagramming, with a little time and practice those who use the diagrams in this book will soon find them an invaluable resource as they work their way through the speech. One caution: obviously no two students, scholars, or teachers of Latin will agree, in every instance, on the syntax of any given word or phrase in a sentence. The present study offers only one interpretation that by no means pretends to be final. If the diagrams that follow inspire those who use them to arrive at conclusions different from those expressed, the book has served its purpose.

M. Tulli Ciceronis

Pro Archia Poeta

Oratio

1 *If there is in me anything of natural talent, gentlemen of the jury, which I realize how slight it is; or if [there is in me] any experience in public speaking, in which I do not deny that I have been somewhat engaged; or if [there is in me] any strategy for the matter here before us, derived from my studies and formal training in the liberal arts, to which I confess that no time of my life has been averse—then of all these things this Aulus Licinius, first and foremost, ought nearly by his own right to claim from me the benefit.*

Notes & Discussion
{1.1–7}

The opening sentence of the EXORDIUM is a finely constructed compound condition with three PROTASES setting up the PERIODIC resolution of the APODOSIS, or main clause. Each of the three conditional clauses is followed first by an adjectival relative clause whose antecedent is in the preceding clause:

ingeni...quod :: exercitatio...in qua :: ratio...a qua

The verb of each relative clause in turn governs its own subordinate clause; *sentio* governs an indirect question, *infiteor* and *confiteor* each govern indirect statements:

sentio quam sit exiguum

infiteor... me...esse versatum

confiteor... tempus abhorruisse

vel in primis..iure suo: while these two adverbial phrases could also be seen as modifying *repetere*, the complementary infinitive of *debet*, they are shown on the diagram here as modifying *debet* because they seem to justify why Archias ought (*debet*) to make the claim (*repetere*), rather than to describe in some way the action of claiming.

prope: the adverb specifically modifies the possessive adjective *suo* and not *iure*, and so the diagram reflects this.

———◆———

1 Si quid est in me ingeni, iudices, quod sentio quam sit exiguum, aut si qua exercitatio dicendi, in qua me non infitior mediocriter esse versatum, aut si huiusce rei ratio aliqua ab optimarum artium studiis ac disciplina profecta, a qua ego nullum confiteor aetatis meae tempus abhorruisse, earum rerum omnium vel in primis hic A. Licinius fructum a me repetere prope suo iure debet.

PROTASES:

si quid est ⇒
    ⌐in me
  ⌐ingeni
    ⌐quod sentio quam sit exiguum

⇒ aut si exercitatio ⇒
    ⌐qua
    ⌐dicendi
    ⌐in qua me non infitior esse versatum
           ⌐mediocriter

⇒ aut si ratio
    ⌐rei
      ⌐huiusce
    ⌐aliqua
    ⌐profecta
      ⌐ab...studiis ac disciplina
        ⌐artium
          ⌐optimarum
    ⌐a qua ego confiteor...tempus abhorruisse
           ⌐nullum
           ⌐aetatis
             ⌐meae

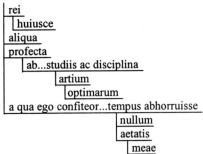

APODOSIS:

A. Licinius fructum   repetere   debet
 ⌐hic   ⌐rerum   ⌐a me   ⌐vel in primis
      ⌐omnium   ⌐iure
      ⌐earum   ⌐suo
                 ⌐prope

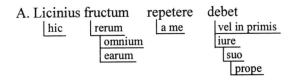

| 2 |

For as far back as possible that my mind is able to reflect on the space of time gone by and to recall the earliest memory of my youth, searching my mind from that point on, I see that this man [Archias] has stood out as most important to me for the purpose of undertaking and embarking upon the course of these studies.

Notes & Discussion
{1.7–12}

The second sentence of the EXORDIUM begins with an adverbial *quoad* clause which is best understood as modifying the participle *repetens* immediately following it. *Hunc* signals the beginning of the main clause, and is the subject accusative of an indirect statement governed by *video*, the verb of the main clause. Cicero BRACKETS the entire main clause by separating *hunc* from the infinitive *exstitisse*, the verb of the indirect statement, with a HYPERBATON of some thirteen words.

mihi: this dative of reference can also be construed with *exstitisse* ("has stood out for me"); but its proximity to *principem* suggests that it should be attributed to the adjective.

———◆———

2 | Nam quoad longissime potest mens mea respicere spatium praeteriti temporis et pueritiae memoriam recordari ultimam, inde usque repetens hunc video mihi principem et ad suscipiendam et ad ingrediendam rationem horum studiorum exstitisse.

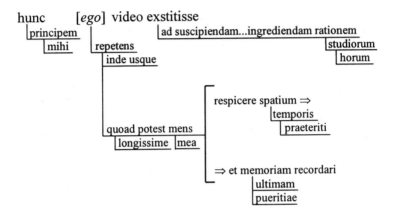

> **3**   *But if this voice, shaped by the encouragement and instructions of this man, has been at times a means of deliverance for some, then certainly to this self-same man, from whom we have received that by which we were able to bring help to some and salvation to others, we ought to provide, as much as lies in our power, aid and deliverance.*

NOTES & DISCUSSION
{1.12–16}

What begins as a simple condition develops into a series of interlocking clauses that build periodically in the PROTASIS and are resolved in the APODOSIS. The position of *vox* at the head of the protasis allows it to bracket first the ablative couple *hortatu praeceptisque* (1) with its resolution of the participle *conformata*, as well as the "double dative" construction of *non nullis saluti* (2), with the periodic resolution of *fuit*, the main verb of the clause, in final position.

Instead of allowing the apodosis to follow immediately after the protasis, Cicero inserts two relative clauses: the first (*a quo id accepimus*) supplies the antecedent (*id*) of the second relative clause that is to follow (*quo ceteris opitulari... possemus*), but precedes its own antecedent, *huic*, the indirect object of the apodosis. But because *huic* is part of the main clause, it cannot occur until after the completion of the *quo...possemus* clause. By arranging the two relative clauses in this way, not only does the *a quo... accepimus* clause look forward to its antecedent in the main clause of the apodosis, but by delaying *huic* until after the *quo...possemus* clause, Cicero can exploit the antithesis of *ceteris... huic*:

Finally, Cicero brings the apodosis to a periodic conclusion with *et opem et salutem ferre debemus.*

———◆———

3 Quod si haec vox huius hortatu praeceptisque conformata non nullis aliquando saluti fuit, a quo id accepimus quo ceteris opitulari et alios servare possemus, huic profecto ipsi, quantum est situm in nobis, et opem et salutem ferre debemus.

PROTASIS:

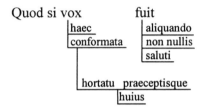

APODOSIS:

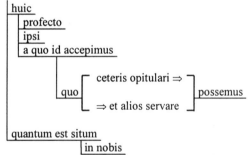

| 4 | *And so that no one, perchance, may wonder that this [oration] is being presented by me in this* |

fashion—because there is in him [i.e. Archias] a certain other sort of endowment of talent and not the [usual] system or discipline of public speaking—[let me say that] not even I have been completely devoted to this one single pursuit.

NOTES & DISCUSSION
{2.16–19}

An awkward sentence to translate smoothly into English, it begins with a negative purpose clause (*ne quis...miretur*) that is resolved by the main clause (*ne nos quidem...dediti fuimus*). Cicero interrupts the communication between these two clauses, however, with the insertion of a *quod* (causal) clause in which he describes the *novum genus dicendi* he intends to use in his defense of Archias. It is very interesting that Cicero uses the same three terms here that he used of himself in the opening sentence (*ingenium, ratio, disciplina*), only now he seems to be making a distinction between what he describes as *quaedam alia facultas ingeni* and the traditional *dicendi ratio aut disciplina*. Note also the CHIASTIC arrangement of nominatives and genitives: *facultas...ingeni :: dicendi ratio aut disciplina*.

———◆———

| 5 | *Indeed, all the arts which pertain to civilized society have a certain common bond, and by a* |

certain, as it were, kindred relationship are connected one to another.

NOTES & DISCUSSION
{2.20–22}

Of the seven sentences that make up the EXORDIUM, this elegant declaration forms the centerpiece of the opening statement and stands out for the simplicity of its syntax, and the philosophical metaphors it contains. As the presence of the conjunction *etenim* indicates, the sentence follows closely on the heels of the previous one, offering further explanation of what has just been said.

———◆———

4 | Ac ne quis a nobis hoc ita dici forte miretur, quod alia quaedam in hoc facultas sit ingeni neque haec dicendi ratio aut disciplina, ne nos quidem huic uni studio penitus umquam dediti fuimus.

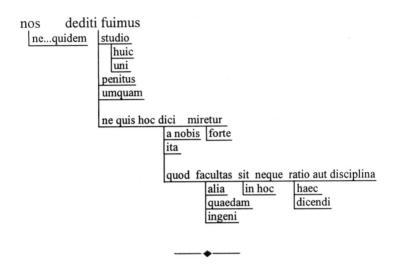

---◆---

5 | Etenim omnes artes quae ad humanitatem pertinent habent quoddam commune vinculum et quasi cognatione quadam inter se continentur.

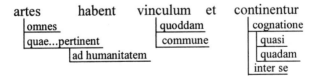

---◆---

6 Sed ne cui vestrum mirum esse videatur, me in quaestione legitima et in iudicio publico, cum res agatur apud praetorem populi Romani, lectissimum virum, et apud severissimos iudices, tanto conventu hominum ac frequentia, hoc uti genere dicendi, quod non modo a consuetudine iudiciorum, verum etiam a forensi sermone abhorreat, quaeso a vobis ut in hac causa mihi detis hanc veniam accommodatam huic reo, vobis, quemadmodum spero, non molestam, ut me pro summo poeta atque eruditissimo homine dicentem, hoc concursu hominum litteratissimorum, hac vestra humanitate, hoc denique praetore exercente iudicium, patiamini de studiis humanitatis ac litterarum paulo loqui liberius, et in eius modi persona quae propter otium ac studium minime in iudiciis periculisque tractata est uti prope novo quodam et inusitato genere dicendi.

But so that it not seem strange to anyone of you that I—in a court of law and in a public trial, with the case being conducted before a praetor of the Roman people, a man elected first at the polls, and before a most strict panel of jurors, [in the presence of] such an assembly and crowd of men—use this style of speaking at odds not only with the customary practice of the courts, but also with the more traditional style of forensic discourse, I ask of you that in this case you grant me this indulgence, one suitable to this defendant, and to you, as I hope, not annoying: namely, that you allow me—pleading on behalf of a most accomplished poet and most learned man, [before] this gathering of most educated men, [in the presence] of your civility, and finally before this praetor conducting the trial—to speak a little more freely about the study of culture and literature, and, assuming a persona of the sort which, on account of its tranquility and studious nature, has been infrequently drawn into to the dangers of a court of justice, to employ a somewhat new and unusual style of speaking.

———◆———

6

quaeso ut detis veniam
  mihi   hanc
a vobis
  in causa   accommodatam non molestam
    hac   reo   vobis
           huic   quemadmodum spero

ut me patiamini loqui   et   uti genere
                de studiis
                       humanitatis ac litterarum
                liberius
                       paulo   novo et inusitato
                                       prope
                                    quodam
                                    dicendi

                in persona
                       modi
                         eius
                       quae tractata est
                                    propter otium
                                       ac studium
dicentem   minime
  pro poeta atque homine   in iudiciis
    summa   eruditissimo   periculisque
  concursu...humanitate...praetore
    hoc   hac   hoc
    hominum   vestra   exercente iudicium

ne mirum esse videatur me uti genere
    cui   hoc
      vestrum   dicendi
                   quod abhorreat
                       a consuetudine...a sermone
                         iudiciorum   forensi
                   in quaestione et in iudicio
                       legitima   publico
                   cum res agatur
                       apud praetorem et iudices
                         populi   severissimos
                           Romani
                         virum
                           lectissimum
                   conventu ac frequentia
                       tanto
                       hominum

| 7 | *And if I perceive that this is being granted and conceded to me by you, I will assuredly cause you* |

to think that this Aulus Licinius is a man who not only, since he [already] is a citizen, ought not to be expunged from the ranks of citizens, but who, even if he were not [already] a citizen, ought to be enrolled [as one].

NOTES & DISCUSSION
{4.37–41}

With a confident assertion of his client's innocence, Cicero concludes the EXORDIUM. The sentence is framed as a simple future-more-vivid condition with a single PROTASIS and an APODOSIS whose main verb, *perficiam*, governs an *ut* clause whose verb, *putetis*, in turn governs a bipartite indirect statement.

mihi a vobis: because indirect object (*mihi*) and ablative of agent (*a vobis*) modify both passive infinitives, they are shown on the diagram between both verbs.

perficiam ut: while the *ut* clause is best translated as the object clause of *perficiam*, it is technically a result clause and therefore is shown on the diagram under *perficiam*.

———◆———

| 8 | *For as soon as Archias departed from boyhood and from those studies by which boyish age is* |

accustomed to be molded into society, he devoted himself to the study of writing.

NOTES & DISCUSSION
{4.42–44}

With this sentence whose straightforward style marks an obvious departure from the rhetorical flourishes and PERIODIC structures that are so characteristic of the EXORDIUM, Cicero begins the NARRATIO.

———◆———

7 Quod si mihi a vobis tribui concedique sentiam, perficiam profecto ut hunc A. Licinium non modo non segregandum, cum sit civis, a numero civium verum etiam, si non esset, putetis asciscendum fuisse.

PROTASIS:

Quod si tribui concedique sentiam
              |mihi
              |a vobis

APODOSIS:

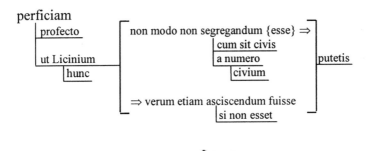

perficiam
       |profecto
       |ut Licinium
              |hunc

non modo non segregandum {esse} ⇒
              |cum sit civis
              |a numero
              |civium
⇒ verum etiam asciscendum fuisse
              |si non esset

putetis

———◆———

8 Nam ut primum ex pueris excessit Archias atque ab eis artibus quibus aetas puerilis ad humanitatem informari solet, se ad scribendi studium contulit.

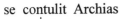
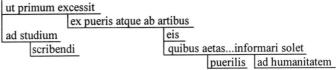

se contulit Archias
       |ut primum excessit
              |ex pueris atque ab artibus
       |ad studium |eis
              |scribendi |quibus aetas...informari solet
                                             |puerilis |ad humanitatem

———◆———

| 9 | *First, at Antioch—for he was born there in a noble station—a city at one time populous and rich and* |

abounding in highly educated men and liberal studies, he quickly began to surpass all men through the renown of his natural talent.

NOTES & DISCUSSION
{4.44–48}

Primum Antiochae: generally, with verbs that pattern with a complementary infinitive, adverbs and adverbial clauses tend to modify the infinitive, as is the case with *celeriter* and *gloria*, both of which modify *antecellere*. It seems that *primum*, however, specifically modifies *coepit*, as it describes that point at which Archias "began," rather than the manner or attendant circumstance under which he "excelled" (*antecellere*); so also with the locative *Antiochae*, which indicates the place where these changes in his life and career began to take place.

———◆———

| 10 | *Subsequently, in the other parts of Asia and all of Greece, his appearances were so celebrated that* |

the expectation of the man surpassed the report of his talent, and the appearance of the man and the admiration [for him] surpassed the expectation [of him].

NOTES & DISCUSSION
{4.48–51}

ut...superaret: the adverbial result clause, while it helps explain *celebrabantur*, is triggered by the adverb *sic*, and so is diagrammed under the adverb.

———◆———

9 | Primum Antiochiae—nam ibi natus est loco
nobili—celebri quondam urbe et copiosa atque
eruditissimis hominibus liberalissimisque studiis adfluenti,
celeriter antecellere omnibus ingeni gloria coepit.

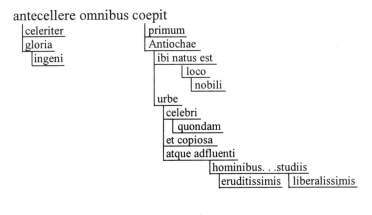

—————◆—————

10 | Post in ceteris Asiae partibus cunctaque Graecia sic
eius adventus celebrabantur ut famam ingeni
exspectatio hominis, exspectationem ipsius adventus
admiratioque superaret.

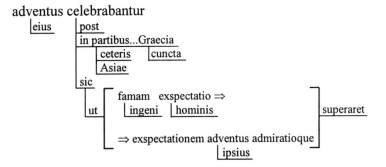

—————◆—————

| 11 | *Italy was at that time full of the Greek arts and disciplines, and these studies even in Latium were being cultivated more enthusiastically then, than now in the same towns; and here at Rome on account of the tranquility of the state they were not being neglected.* |

NOTES & DISCUSSION
{5.52–55}

Cicero now moves from Greece to Italy, and lands Archias in the southern region of the peninsula, an area originally settled by Greek colonists and for that reason referred to as Magna Graecia. The sentence is composed of three independent clauses that progress from southern to central Italy (*et in Latio*), and from there to Rome (*hic Romae*). The PARATACTIC arrangement of the clauses, plus the absence of any subordination, gives equal weight to each.

Graecarum: construe the genitive with both *artium* and *disciplinarum.*

———◆———

| 12 | *Therefore, the people of Tarentum and Locri and Rhegium and Naples gifted him with citizenship and other rewards, and all men who were able to make any judgment at all about natural talents deemed him worthy of their acquaintance and hospitality.* |

NOTES & DISCUSSION
{5.56–59}

This compound sentence contains two independent clauses and an adjectival relative clause, all of which share similar periodic structure. Each begins with the subject at the head of its clause and verb in final position, the only exception being *hunc* which occurs at the beginning of the entire sentence and functions as the direct object (1) of *donarunt* in the first independent clause; and also (2) of *existimarunt* in the second, taking as its predicate complement *dignum* (with an understood *esse*).

———◆———

11 Erat Italia tum plena Graecarum artium ac disciplinarum, studiaque haec et in Latio vehementius tum colebantur quam nunc isdem in oppidis, et hic Romae propter tranquillitatem rei publicae non neglegebantur.

Erat Italia plena ⇒
⌊tum   ⌊artium ac disciplinarum
                    ⌊Graecarum

⇒ studiaque colebantur ⇒
    ⌊haec   ⌊et in Latio
                    ⌊vehementius tum
                        ⌊quam nunc in oppidis
                                ⌊isdem

⇒ et non neglegabantur
                ⌊hic
                ⌊Romae
                ⌊propter tranquillitatem
                    ⌊rei publicae

——◆——

12 Itaque hunc et Tarentini et Locrenses et Regini et Neapolitani civitate ceterisque praemiis donarunt, et omnes qui aliquid de ingeniis poterant iudicare cognitione atque hospitio dignum existimarunt.

hunc et T. et L. et R. et N. donarunt ⇒
                        ⌊civitate...praemiis
                            ⌊ceteris

⇒ et omnes dignum [*esse*] hunc existimarunt
            ⌊   ⌊cognitione atque hospitio

        ⌊qui aliquid poterant iudicare
                    ⌊de ingeniis

——◆——

13 *When, through the great popularity of his reputation, he was already known to men, though he had never met them, he came to Rome in the consulship of Marius and Catulus.*

NOTES & DISCUSSION
{5.59–61}

The sentence opens with an adverbial ablative phrase postponing the conjunction *cum* that ought to have introduced the clause, modifying the adjective *notus* which is delayed until the end of the clause to juxtapose it with *absentibus*.

———◆———

14 *First, he struck up a relationship with those consuls, of whom [the former] one [was able to offer] the greatest achievements to be written about, the other was able to offer not only his accomplishments, but also his attention and his ears.*

NOTES & DISCUSSION
{5.61–64}

ad scribendum: *ad* + the gerund, which expresses purpose, is an adverbial construction and so is shown under *adhibere*. Its placement in the sentence, bracketed by Marius' *res... maximas,* indicates that it must also be understood with the *res gestas* of Catulus, but not with *studium* or *auris.*

———◆———

15 *Immediately thereupon the Luculli, although Archias was even then still wearing his boyhood toga praetexta, received him at their house.*

NOTES & DISCUSSION
{5.63–65}

In this simple sentence, Cicero begins with the subject of the main clause, but suspends its resolution with the insertion of the *cum* clause.

———◆———

13 Hac tanta celebritate famae cum esset iam
absentibus notus, Romam venit Mario consule et
Catulo.

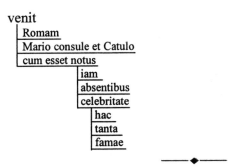

```
venit
  │ Romam
  │ Mario consule et Catulo
  │ cum esset notus
            │ iam
            │ absentibus
            │ celebritate
                    │ hac
                    │ tanta
                    │ famae
```

———◆———

14 Nactus est primum consules eos quorum alter res ad
scribendum maximas, alter cum res gestas tum
etiam studium atque auris adhibere posset.

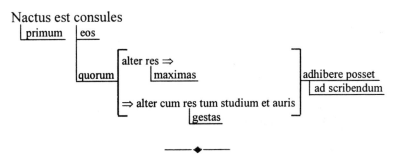

```
Nactus est consules
  │ primum   │ eos
                    ┌ alter res ⇒
                    │         │ maximas        │ adhibere posset
            │ quorum                              │ ad scribendum
                    │
                    └ ⇒ alter cum res tum studium et auris
                                    │ gestas
```

———◆———

15 Statim Luculli, cum praetextatus etiam tum Archias
esset, eum domum suam receperunt.

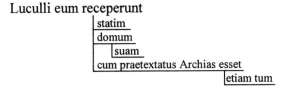

```
Luculli eum receperunt
              │ statim
              │ domum
                    │ suam
              │ cum praetextatus Archias esset
                                    │ etiam tum
```

———◆———

16	*This showed not only the brilliance of his talent and education, but also of his character and virtue,*

namely that the house, which first showed favor to him in his youth, was the same one that was still most welcome to him as an old man.

NOTES & DISCUSSION
{5.65–68}

Hoc, the subject of *dedit*, anticipates the *ut* clause, which Cicero interrupts with the insertion of the relative *quae* clause, immediately following its antecedent *domus*. Cicero ends the sentence with a rhetorically balanced CHIASMUS that exploits the fact that *favit*, the verb of the *quae* clause, and *familiarissima*, the subject complement of *domus...eadem esset*, both pattern with the dative case:

adulescentiae prima favit...esset familiarissima senectuti

verb
nominative adjective
dative noun

ut...senectuti: this clause stands in apposition to *hoc*, and is therefore construed with it in this diagram.

——◆——

17	*He was at that time on good terms with Quintus Metellus, the celebrated Numidicus, and his son*

Pius; he was listened to by Marcus Aemilius; he lived with Quintus Catulus, both father and son; by Lucius Crassus he was greatly esteemed.

NOTES & DISCUSSION
{6.69–72}

Four brief, PARATACTICALLY arranged independent clauses that read like a virtual "who's who" register of Rome's most distinguished families. The simplicity of the syntax highlights the names, but note how Cicero shifts constructions in the fourth clause, placing *colebatur* in final position to signal closure.

——◆——

16 Dedit etiam hoc non solum lumen ingeni ac litterarum, verum etiam naturae atque virtutis ut domus, quae huius adulescentiae prima favit, eadem esset familiarissima senectuti.

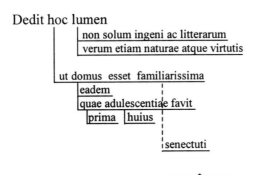

Dedit hoc lumen
non solum ingeni ac litterarum
verum etiam naturae atque virtutis

ut domus esset familiarissima
eadem
quae adulescentiae favit
prima huius

senectuti

---◆---

17 Erat temporibus illis iucundus Q. Metello, illi Numidico, et eius Pio filio, audiebatur a M. Aemilio, vivebat cum Q. Catulo et patre et filio, a L. Crasso colebatur.

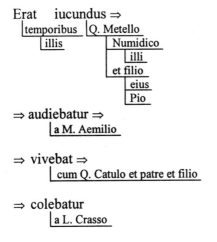

Erat iucundus ⇒
temporibus Q. Metello
illis Numidico
illi
et filio
eius
Pio

⇒ audiebatur ⇒
a M. Aemilio

⇒ vivebat ⇒
cum Q. Catulo et patre et filio

⇒ colebatur
a L. Crasso

---◆---

| **18** | *Since he held the Luculli and Drusus and the Octavii and Cato and the entire house of the Hortensii bound by close social ties, he was treated with the greatest honor, because not only did those cultivate him, who were eager to learn or hear something, but also if any by chance pretended to be eager.* |

NOTES & DISCUSSION
{6.72–76}

The list of Archias' patrons continues. Although the sentence begins with a subordinate *cum* clause, Cicero postpones *cum* for some fourteen words in order to emphasize the names. The brief main clause, consisting only of a single verb (*adficiebatur*) and ablative modifier (*summo honore*), is followed by a *quod* (causal) clause whose two relative clauses are set in balance by *non solum...verum etiam.*

————◆————

| **19** | *Meanwhile, after a sufficient interval of time had passed, when he had gone with Marcus Lucullus to Sicily, and when from that province with the self-same Lucullus he departed, he came to Heraclea.* |

NOTES & DISCUSSION
{6.76–79}

The sentence contains an interesting play on *cum*, which occurs four times: twice as the subordinate clause marker, twice as the preposition. While this may seem a bit clunky stylistically, the effect was deliberate. Both subordinate clauses are bracketed by their clause markers and verbs (*cum ...profectus* :: *cum...decederet*) and in turn bracket a CHIASTIC arrangement of prepositional phrases (*cum M. Lucullo in Siciliam...ex ea provincia cum eodem Lucullo*). This seemingly wordy repetition emphasizes Archias' position on Lucullus' provincial staff and allows Cicero a second opportunity to drop the name of the influential patron.

Cum esset cum L. in Siciliam profectus et cum ex provincia cum L. decederet

————◆————

18 Lucullos vero et Drusum et Octavios et Catonem et totam Hortensiorum domum devinctam consuetudine cum teneret, adficiebatur summo honore, quod eum non solum colebant, qui aliquid percipere atque audire studebant, verum etiam si qui forte simulabant.

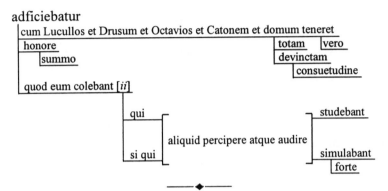

19 Interim satis longo intervallo, cum esset cum M. Lucullo in Siciliam profectus et cum ex ea provincia cum eodem Lucullo decederet, venit Heracleam.

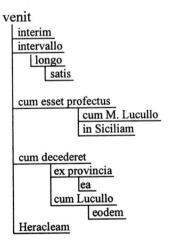

| 20 | *And since this was a city with full civic privileges under the law, he wished to be enrolled [as a citizen] in this city, and this—since he was thought to be worthy on his own merits, and with the support and influence of the Luculli—he obtained from the Heracleans.* |

NOTES & DISCUSSION
{6.79–83}

The two halves of this compound sentence at first appear to be structurally parallel, as each begins with a *cum* clause followed by the main clause. But this syntactic balance breaks down in the second half of the sentence. In the first half, the initial *cum* clause is causal; in the second half, however, the main clause following the *cum* clause is introduced by *tum*, indicating that Cicero has shifted to the correlative *cum...tum* construction, which is usually either temporal ("when...then") or copulative ("both...and"), neither of which seems to be what is needed here. But there is still something inherently correlative about the progression of ideas between the *cum* clause and the main clause that would support the use of *tum* here. Cicero gives three reasons why Archias obtained (*impetravit*) citizenship at Heraclea: the first reason (his own *dignitas*) is given in the *cum* clause;   the second and third (the *auctoritas* and *gratia* of Lucullus) are given in the *tum* clause. The political significance of the terms *dignitas*, *auctoritas*, and *gratia*, and their relevance as contributing factors influencing the decision to award citizenship, would have been obvious to a Roman audience.

aequissimo: construe the superlative adjective with both *iure* and *foedere*, which are best translated as a single idea, an example of HENDIADYS.

per se: the prepositional phrase modifies an understood *esse*, a complementary infinitive with *putaretur*, which has been supplied on the diagram.

Luculli: because the genitive modifies *auctoritate* and *gratia* it is shown on the diagram under both ablatives.

———◆———

20 Quae cum esset civitas aequissimo iure ac foedere, ascribi se in eam civitatem voluit idque, cum ipse per se dignus putaretur, tum auctoritate et gratia Luculli ab Heracliensibus impetravit.

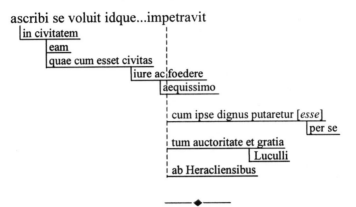

| 21 | *Citizenship was granted by the law of Silvanus and Carbo: "If any persons had been enrolled among* |

confederated cities; if at that time when the law was being passed they had maintained a residence in Italy; and if within sixty days they had registered with the praetor."

NOTES & DISCUSSION
{7.83–86}

What the original wording of the law was we have no way of knowing, but whenever Cicero paraphrases a law in one of his orations, the paraphrase takes much the same form as this one, so it may be safe to assume that the way laws appeared on the books, as it were, was much as we see here: a series of PROTASES laying down the conditions that had to be met in order to be in compliance with a law. Whether or not laws were even written with APODOSES is hard to say, but here Cicero supplies his own (*data est civitas*).

in Italia: the prepositional phrase refers to where one would have had (*habuisset*) a *domicilium*, and not to where the law was passed (*ferebatur*).

———◆———

21 Data est civitas Silvani lege et Carbonis: SI QUI
FOEDERATIS CIVITATIBUS ASCRIPTI FUISSENT, SI TUM
CUM LEX FEREBATUR IN ITALIA DOMICILIUM HABUISSENT ET
SI SEXAGINTA DIEBUS APUD PRAETOREM ESSENT PROFESSI.

PROTASES:

si qui ascripti fuissent ⇒
    |civitatibus
      |foederatis

⇒ si domicilium habuissent ⇒
          |tum
          |cum lex ferebatur
          |in Italia

⇒ et si essent professi
      |diebus
        |sexaginta
      |apud praetorem

APODOSIS:

Data est civitas
    |lege
      |Silvani et Carbonis

| 22 | *Since he maintained a domicile at Rome for many years already, he registered with the praetor Quintus Metellus, his most intimate friend.* |

Notes & Discussion
{7.87–89}

iam: because of its position between *multos* and *annos* the adverb should be construed with this phrase, and so appears in the diagram under *multos* instead of *haberet*.

Q. Metellum, familiarissimum suum: the name *Q. Metellum* is in APPOSITION to *praetorem*, as also is *familiarissimum*, the superlative adjective used here as a SUBSTANTIVE (i.e., as a noun), and therefore able to be modified by the possessive adjective *suum*.

———◆———

| 23 | *There is present a man with the utmost authority and conscientiousness and integrity, Marcus Lucullus, who says that he does not think, but knows; that he did not [merely] hear, but [actually] saw; that he was not only present, but had taken part [in the process].* |

Notes & Discussion
{8.93–95}

The main clause begins emphatically with *adest*, stressing Lucullus' presence in court. The subject and its APPOSITIVE, *vir…M. Lucullus*, bracket three ablatives of description. In the *qui* clause that follows, the "bookend" structure of *se*, the subject of the indirect statement, and the governing verb, *dicit*, in final position, brackets a TRICOLON of ANTITHETICAL pairs of infinitives arranged in ASYNDETON.

summa: although on the diagram it is attributed only to *auctoritate*, the superlative adjective should be applied to the entire tricolon of ablatives, all of which are feminine and singular, as is *summa*.

———◆———

22 Cum hic domicilium Romae multos iam annos haberet, professus est apud praetorem Q. Metellum, familiarissimum suum.

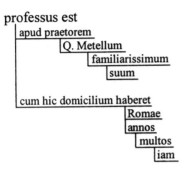

professus est
apud praetorem
    Q. Metellum
      familiarissimum
        suum
cum hic domicilium haberet
    Romae
    annos
      multos
        iam

———◆———

23 Adest vir summa auctoritate et religione et fide, M. Lucullus, qui se non opinari sed scire, non audisse sed vidisse, non interfuisse sed egisse dicit.

Adest vir

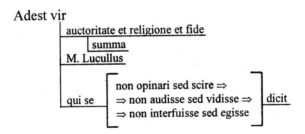

auctoritate et religione et fide
    summa
M. Lucullus
qui se — non opinari sed scire ⇒ ⇒ non audisse sed vidisse ⇒ ⇒ non interfuisse sed egisse — dicit

———◆———

| 24 | *There are present Heraclean delegates, most respectable men; they have come for the sake of* |

this trial with mandates and with public testimony, who say that he was enrolled [as a citizen] at Heraclea.

NOTES & DISCUSSION
{8.95–98}

This sentence, in both structure and language, is meant to recall the previous sentence, as Cicero begins with the emphatic placement of *adsunt* in first position, followed by the subject (*Heraclienses legati*) modified by the APPOSITIVE *nobilissimi homines*. In order to avoid strict parallelism between this sentence and the previous one, however, Cicero expands the main clause with the addition of a second (*huius...venerunt*). Note how the "bookend" placement *adsunt...venerunt*, brackets the two main clauses. Just as in the previous sentence, Cicero concludes with a relative *qui* clause whose main verb, *dicunt*, occurs in final position and governs an indirect statement.

———◆———

| 25 | *At this point do you desire the public records of the Heracleans, which we all know to have* |

perished with the burning of the Tabularium [records office] in the Italian War?

NOTES & DISCUSSION
{8.99–100}

incenso tabulario: while the ablative noun, *tabulario*, is being modified by the ablative participle *incenso*, because the entire construction forms an ablative absolute, an adverbial modifier, both words appear as a single modifier on the same line.

———◆———

| 24 | Adsunt Heraclienses legati, nobilissimi homines, huius iudici causa cum mandatis et cum publico testimonio venerunt, qui hunc ascriptum Heracleae esse dicunt. |

testimonio venerunt, qui hunc ascriptum Heracleae esse dicunt.

Adsunt legati ⇒

    | Heraclienses
    | homines
        | nobilissimi

    | qui hunc ascriptum esse dicunt
            | Heracleae

⇒ venerunt

    | causa
        | iudici
            | huius
    | cum mandatis
    | et cum testimonio
            | publico

———◆———

| 25 | Hic tu tabulas desideras Heracliensium publicas, quas Italico bello incenso tabulario interisse scimus omnes? |

omnes?

tu tabulas   desideras?

    | Heracliensium | hic
    | publicas
    | quas interisse scimus [nos]
                | bello | omnes
                    | Italico
                | incenso tabulario

———◆———

> **26**   *It is ridiculous to say nothing in regard to those things which we have, to seek those things which we are not able to have, and to be silent about the memory of men, [yet] to demand the memory of written records, and, although you have the pledge of a most distinguished man, the sworn oath and faith of a most respectable town, to reject those things which can in no way be falsified, [yet] to desire public records, which you the self-same person say are accustomed to be corrupted.*

NOTES & DISCUSSION
{8.100–106}

One of the finest sentences of the entire speech for its clarity of expression, the structural symmetry of its clauses, and carefully balanced antitheses. It begins with *est ridiculum*, the patronizing, contemptuous predicate of the main clause, followed by a series of six infinitive clauses arranged in a TRICOLON of antithetical pairs. The first member is arranged CHIASTICALLY (*quae habemus* + infinitive :: infinitive + *quae habemus*):

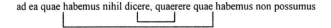

In the second member, the arrangement of the elements of the two clauses is parallel (genitive plural + *memoria(m)* + infinitive):

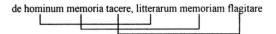

The third member, like the second, is also arranged in parallel word order: accusative plural + relative clause (modifying the accusative plural) + infinitive:

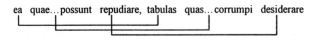

26 Est ridiculum ad ea quae habemus nihil dicere, quaerere quae habere non possumus, et de hominum memoria tacere, litterarum memoriam flagitare et, cum habeas amplissimi viri religionem, integerrimi municipi ius iurandum fidemque, ea quae depravari nullo modo possunt repudiare, tabulas quas idem dicis solere corrumpi desiderare.

```
                    ┌  nihil dicere ⇒
                    │      └ ad ea
                    │          └ quae habemus
                    │
                    │  ⇒ quaerere quae habere non possumus ⇒
                    │
                    │  ⇒ et tacere ⇒
                    │      └ de memoria
                    │          └ hominum
                    │
  Est ridiculum ────┤  ⇒ flagitare memoriam ⇒
                    │          └ litterarum
                    │
                    │  ⇒ et repudiare ea ⇒
                    │              └ quae depravari non possunt
                    │
                    │      cum habeas religionem ius iurandum  fidemque
                    │              └ viri                  └ municipi
                    │                  └ amplissimi            └ integerrimi
                    │
                    │  ⇒ desiderare tabulas
                    └          └ quas [tu] dicis solere corrumpi
                                    └ idem
```

<table>
<tr><td>27</td><td>Or did he not maintain a residence in Rome, who for so many years before citizenship was granted</td></tr>
</table>

had established the seat of all his possessions and fortunes at Rome?

NOTES & DISCUSSION
{9.107–109}

A brief main clause followed by a relative *qui* clause anticipated by the demonstrative pronoun *is*. Note the repetition of the locative *Romae* in both main and dependent clauses, emphasizing that Archias was well-established in the city in compliance with the *Lex Plautia Papiria*.

———◆———

<table>
<tr><td>28</td><td>On the contrary, he did register in those records which are the only ones from that registration</td></tr>
</table>

and that board of praetors that still have the force of public records.

NOTES & DISCUSSION
{9.109–112}

The main clause under analysis here does not include the question that prompts it (*An non est professus?*). But in answering his own question, Cicero cannot avoid playing with the diction: *non est professus? Immo vero...professus... professione.* As in the previous sentence, the brief main clause is followed by an extended relative *quae* clause anticipated by the demonstrative *eis*.

———◆———

27 An domicilium Romae non habuit is qui tot annis ante civitatem datam sedem omnium rerum ac fortunarum suarum Romae conlocavit?

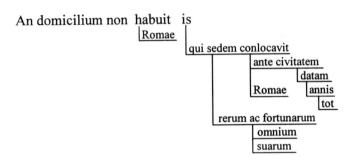

An domicilium non habuit is
             Romae
                qui sedem conlocavit
                      ante civitatem
                            datam
                      Romae   annis
                              tot
                  rerum ac fortunarum
                    omnium
                    suarum

28 An non est professus? Immo vero eis tabulis professus quae solae ex illa professione conlegioque praetorum obtinent publicarum tabularum auctoritatem.

professus [*est*]
    immo vero
    tabulis
      eis
      quae obtinent auctoritatem
        solae   tabularum
                    publicarum
        ex professione conlegioque
          illa   praetorum

| 29 | *For although the records of Appius were said to have been kept somewhat carelessly, [and although] the unreliability of Gabinius—as long as he was safe from prosecution—[and] his ruin—after his condemnation—had violated all the confidence of his records, Metellus, a man most scrupulous and temperate of all men, was of so great diligence that to Lucius Lentulus the praetor and to the jurors he came and said that he was troubled by the erasure of a single name.* |

Notes & Discussion
{9.112–118}

The sentence begins with an extended *cum* (concessive) clause in which Cicero introduces, and then dismisses, Appius and Gabinius, two of the PRAETORS of 89 B.C. Cicero deals with these two men together in the subordinate clause, in order to contrast them with Metellus, whom he introduces in the main clause (note also the shift of case from the genitive for Appius and Gabinius, to the nominative for Metellus). The main clause in which Metellus appears is brief, but important to the structure of the whole sentence, as it serves not only to resolve the initial *cum* clause, but also governs an *ut* clause of result, in which Cicero explains at length why Metellus was *sanctissimus modestissimusque omnium*.

———◆———

29 | Nam, cum Appi tabulae neglegentius adservatae dicerentur, Gabini, quam diu incolumis fuit, levitas, post damnationem calamitas omnem tabularum fidem resignasset, Metellus, homo sanctissimus modestissimusque omnium, tanta diligentia fuit ut ad L. Lentulum praetorem et ad iudices venerit et unius nominis litura se commotum esse dixerit.

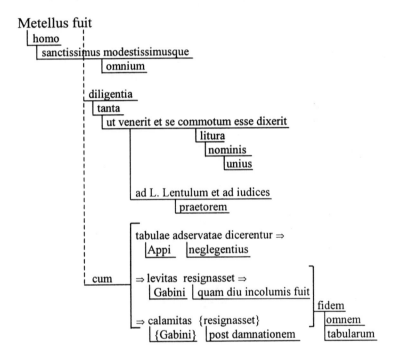

| 30 | *And since these things are so, why is it that you should be in doubt about his citizenship, especially since he had been enrolled [as a citizen] in other cities?* |

NOTES & DISCUSSION
{10.119–121}

The sentence begins with the formulaic phrase *quae cum ita sint*, followed by the somewhat wordy *quid est quod...dubitetis* construction of the main clause. Cicero exhibits similar verbosity in the *cum* clause with the addition of *praesertim* and the artificial separation of *aliis* from the prepositional phrase *in civitatibus* by the insertion of the adverb *quoque*.

——◆——

| 31 | *For [at a time] when to many ordinary men— and those endowed with either no skill or some insignificant one—men in [Magna] Graecia were offering citizenship, [am] I [really to] believe that the Rhegians, or the Locrians, or the Neapolitans, or the Tarentines would not have been willing to bestow upon a man endowed with the greatest renown of talent that which they were accustomed to bestow upon stage actors?* |

NOTES & DISCUSSION
{10.121–126}

The sentence begins with a circumstantial *cum* clause whose indirect object and its modifiers occupy the first part of the clause. The adjective *multis*, functioning as a SUBSTANTIVE, is modified on one side by *mediocribus*, on the other by the participle *praeditis*. The main clause that follows, on the other hand, begins with a series of accusatives that will become the subjects of the indirect statement governed by *credo*. Cicero delays the resolution of the indirect statement by inserting a relative *quod* clause that anticipates its antecedent, *id*, the direct object of the indirect statement. The verb of the indirect statement, *noluisse,* is postponed to final position by the insertion of its indirect object, *huic...praedito*, a dative phrase that stands in direct antithesis to *multis...praeditis* at the beginning of the sentence.

——◆——

30 Quae cum ita sint, quid est quod de eius civitate dubitetis, praesertim cum aliis quoque in civitatibus fuerit ascriptus?

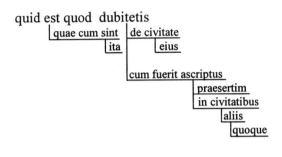

---◆---

31 Etenim cum mediocribus multis et aut nulla aut humili aliqua arte praeditis gratuito civitatem in Graecia homines impertiebant, Reginos credo aut Locrensis aut Neapolitanos aut Tarentinos, quod scaenicis artificibus largiri solebant, id huic summa ingeni praedito gloria noluisse!

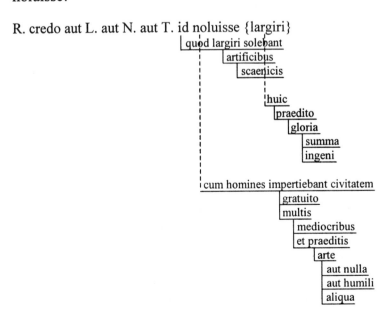

---◆---

| 32 | *Well, what about when other men—not only after citizenship had been granted, but even after the [passing of the]Papian Law—had slipped into the registers of other municipalities by any means [possible], will this man, who does not even use those [registers] in which he is enrolled because he always wished that he be [considered] a Heraclean, be rejected?* |

NOTES & DISCUSSION
{10.126–131}

The focus of this sentence is the antithesis of *ceteri*, the subject of the *cum* clause, and *hic*, the subject of the main clause. The *cum* clause is periodically arranged with *ceteri* in first position and its verb, *inrepserunt*, at the end. Bracketed within this "bookend" composition are three prepositional phrases, the first two balanced by *non modo...sed etiam*. Likewise, although the main clause consists only of two words (*hic reicietur*), the subject and verb are separated by two relative clauses and a *quod* (causal) clause, creating a HYPERBATON of some fifteen words.

———◆———

32 Quid? cum ceteri non modo post civitatem datam sed etiam post legem Papiam aliquo modo in eorum municipiorum tabulas inrepserunt, hic qui ne utitur quidem illis in quibus est scriptus, quod semper se Heracliensem esse voluit, reicietur?

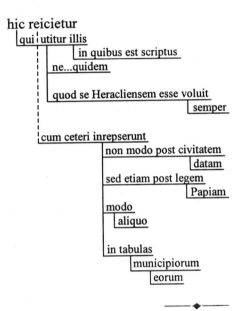

33 | *For it is [hardly] a secret that under the last censors he was with that most illustrious commander, Lucius Lucullus, with the army; that under the previous [censors] he was with that same man [when he was] quaestor in Asia; that under the first [censors], Julius [Caesar] and Licinius [Crassus], no part of the populace had been registered in a census.*

NOTES & DISCUSSION
{11.131–135}

The governing construction of this sentence recalls that of no. 26 (*est ridiculum...*): the predicate of the main clause consists of *est* + a neuter adjective, raising the expectation of one or more subjective infinitive clauses. In this case what follows are three accusative + infinitive clauses, each introduced by an ablative or ablative phrase that establishes the relative chronology of the three clauses in terms of the last three times the census was taken at Rome (*proximis censoribus... superioribus...primis*). And while the formal symmetry of these three chronological terms raises the expectation of further parallelism in the three clauses they introduce, Cicero does not fulfill it. While the first two clauses share the same accusative subject (*hunc*), and require *fuisse* as their verb, in the third clause Cicero shifts constructions completely, introducing a new subject and changing the voice of the infinitive. The reason for the change, perhaps, is that the first two clauses account for Archias' failure to be recorded in the last two censuses due to his absence from Rome and his service on Lucullus' provincial staff; in the third clause, Archias' failure to appear on the register of the first census was due not to his absence from Rome, but rather to the fact that the census for that year was woefully incomplete.

33 Est enim obscurum proximis censoribus hunc cum clarissimo imperatore L. Lucullo apud exercitum fuisse, superioribus cum eodem quaestore fuisse in Asia, primis Iulio et Crasso nullam populi partem esse censam.

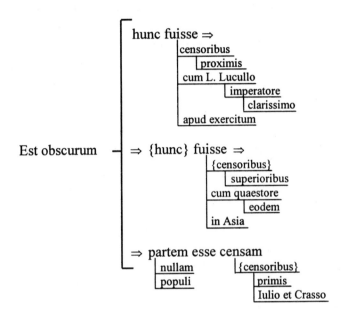

| 34 | *But since the census does not confirm citizenship—and in fact merely indicates that whoever happened to be recorded was at that time* |

conducting himself in the manner of a citizen—during those times he, whom you charge to have been not even in his own opinion entitled to the rights of Roman citizens, both often made a will [in accordance with] our laws, and entered into the inheritances of Roman citizens, and was recommended to the treasury for a bonus by Lucius Lucullus the proconsul.

NOTES & DISCUSSION
{11.135–142}

The sentence begins with a bipartite causal clause (*quoniam*) followed by three independent clauses. The verb of the second member of the *quoniam* clause, *indicat*, governs an accusative + infinitive indirect statement (*eum...se...gessisse*) that is interrupted by the insertion of a relative clause. The first of the three main clauses is introduced by the temporal ablative phrase *eis temporibus*, which should be understood with all three clauses. The subject of the first clause, *is*, is separated from the predicate of its clause by the insertion of a relative clause that governs an accusative + infinitive construction (*quem...esse versatum*). Once the relative clause ends, however, the delivery of the main clauses resumes and continues without any further interruption. While the repetition of *et...et...et* raises the expectation of parallelism or PERIODIC structure, Cicero seems to deliberately avoid it.

———◆———

34 Sed, quoniam census non ius civitatis confirmat ac tantum modo indicat eum, qui sit census, ita se iam tum gessisse pro cive, eis temporibus is quem tu criminaris ne ipsius quidem iudicio in civium Romanorum iure esse versatum et testamentum saepe fecit nostris legibus, et adiit hereditates civium Romanorum, et in beneficiis ad aerarium delatus est a L. Lucullo pro consule.

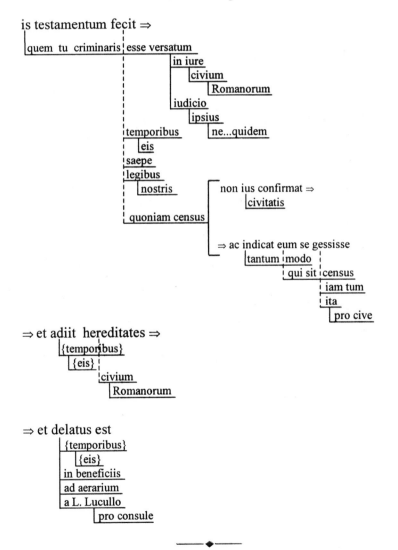

| 35 | *Or do you suppose that what we say on a daily basis in so great a variety of circumstances* |

would be available to us, unless we cultivated our minds by means of formal education, or that our minds could endure such great conflict, unless we relaxed them by means of this same education?

NOTES & DISCUSSION
{12.147–150}

The particle *an* usually follows *utrum* and introduces the second member of an alternative question. When *an* appears alone, as here, it usually means that the first alternative is so obvious as to need no articulation at all, and therefore the particle lends a tone of indignation or surprise to the expressed question. *Existimas* governs two accusative + infinitive clauses, set in formal balance by the repetition of *aut...aut*, and sharing nearly parallel structures (*aut suppetere...posse ...nisi...excolamus* :: *aut ferre...posse...nisi relaxemus*). Cicero achieves variation by using the relative noun clause (*quod...dicamus*) for the subject of *posse* in the first clause, and *animos* as the subject in the second, then alternating the two complementary infinitives, from intransitive (*suppetere*) in the first clause, to transitive (*ferre*) in the second. The two *nisi* clauses are even more symmetrical than their governing infinitive clauses, with *eos* as the direct object of *relaxemus* in the second picking up *animos* in the first, the repetition of the ablative *doctrina* in both clauses, and first person plural verbs in final position.

————◆————

35 An tu existimas aut suppetere nobis posse quod cotidie dicamus in tanta varietate rerum, nisi animos nostros doctrina excolamus, aut ferre animos tantam posse contentionem, nisi eos doctrina eadem relaxemus?

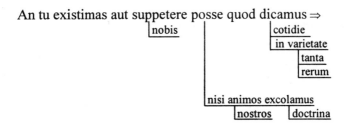

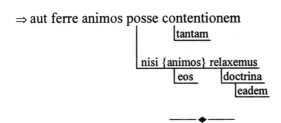

| 36 | *Let it shame others if any have so buried themselves in literature that they are not able to* |

produce anything from these [studies] for the common good, nor to bring forth [anything] into the scrutiny and the light [of day]; why, on the other hand, should it cause me shame, gentlemen of the jury, who for so many years have lived my life in such a way that my leisure has never distracted me from the hour [of need] or the interest of anyone, nor has [my pursuit of] pleasure called me away from it, nor, finally, has sleep [ever] held me back [from helping anyone]?

Notes & Discussion
{12.151–157}

The structure of the two independent clauses that make up this sentence focuses on the antithesis of how others (*ceteros*) may be negatively affected by the time they devote to the study of literature, and Cicero's (*me*) ability to derive nothing but positive results from a life of learning. Both clauses share the same basic framework. In the first clause, *ceteros*, the direct object of *pudeat*, occurs emphatically in first position; while *pudeat* is usually an impersonal verb, here it is taking as its subject the *si qui...abdiderunt* clause which contains the particle *ita* that anticipates an *ut* clause of result. Because the second clause, unlike the first, is a question, the interrogative pronoun *quid* functions as the subject of *pudeat*; like *ceteros* in the first clause, *me,* the direct object of *pudeat*, also occurs emphatically at the head of its clause, followed by an adjectival relative clause modifying it and containing the particle *ita*, anticipating an *ut* clause of result. The two result clauses, while they do not mirror each other to the extent that their governing clauses do, share similar parallel features. In the first *ut* clause, *nihil possint* governs two complementary infinitives (*adferre...proferre*) balanced by *neque...neque*; the second *ut* clause contains a TRICOLON of short, symmetrical clauses, set in formal parallelism by the ANAPHORA of *aut...aut...aut.*

————◆————

36 | Ceteros pudeat, si qui ita se litteris abdiderunt ut nihil possint ex eis neque ad communem adferre fructum neque in aspectum lucemque proferre; me autem quid pudeat qui tot annos ita vivo, iudices, ut a nullius umquam me tempore aut commodo aut otium meum abstraxerit aut voluptas avocarit aut denique somnus retardarit?

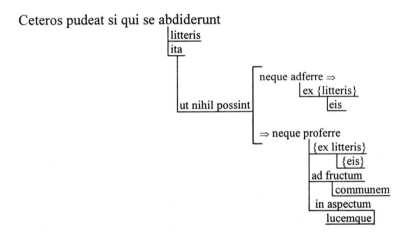

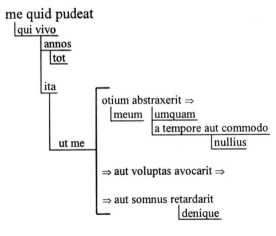

| 37 | *Wherefore, who at last would rebuke me, or who could justly be angry with me if, as much time as* |

is conceded by others for the purpose of attending to their own affairs, [if] as much [time] as is conceded for the purpose of celebrating festival days for the games, [if] as much [time] as is conceded to other pleasures and relaxations of the mind and body, [if] as much [time] as others devote to dinner parties, [if], finally, as much [time] as others devote to gaming, [if] as much [time] as they devote to playing ball, that much time I myself, for myself, should apply to the cultivation of these pursuits?

NOTES & DISCUSSION
{13.157–164}

It is generally Cicero's practice, when composing conditional sentences, to begin with the PROTASIS and conclude with the APODOSIS. In this sentence, however, it is obvious that the compound protasis is intended to carry the weight of the argument, and so Cicero dispenses with the apodosis first. It is also possible that Cicero wanted to cast the sentence as a question and so decided to begin with the apodosis, in which he repeats the interrogative pronoun twice, which also allows him to play with the juxtaposition of pronouns (*quis...me...aut quis mihi*). The protasis is an extended *quantum...tantum* correlative construction whose six *quantum* clauses can be subdivided into two TRICOLA. The structure of the first tricolon is *quantum* (= subject) + *conceditur* + *ceteris* (= dative of agent). The tricolon is introduced by the ANAPHORA of *quantum*, followed only in the first clause by *ceteris*; Cicero delays *temporum*, a partitive genitive modifying *quantum*, until the end of the third clause, along with *conceditur*. In the second tricolon, Cicero shifts from the passive to the active voice: *quantum* (= direct object) + *alii* (= subject) + *tribuunt*. In the *tantum* clause, Cicero tries to accommodate the syntax of both tricola by using both the dative and nominative of the personal pronoun: *mihi egomet* responding to *ceteris* and *alii*.

———◆———

37 Quare quis tandem me reprehendat, aut quis mihi iure suscenseat si, quantum ceteris ad suas res obeundas, quantum ad festos dies ludorum celebrandos, quantum ad alias voluptates et ad ipsam requiem animi et corporis conceditur temporum, quantum alii tribuunt tempestivis conviviis, quantum denique alveolo, quantum pilae, tantum mihi egomet ad haec studia recolenda sumpsero?

PROTASIS:

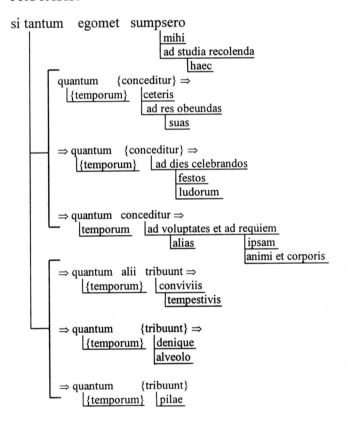

APODOSIS:

quis me reprehendat aut quis mihi suscenseat
⎿tandem ⎿iure

| 38 | *And by so much the more is this to be conceded to me, because from these studies also grows this capacity for public speaking which, however great [or small] it is in me, has never failed the dangers of my friends.* |

Notes & Discussion
{13.164–167}

haec...oratio et facultas: the use of the demonstrative *haec* with *oratio* may identify *oratio* as the antecedent of the following *quae* clause were it not for *facultas*. While it may be that the phrase *oratio et facultas* forms a HENDIADYS that is then described by the following *quae* clause, for practical reasons the *quae* clause is diagrammed under *facultas*, the noun closest to it.

———◆———

| 39 | *And if this [capacity] seems to anyone [to be] somewhat trivial, I certainly am aware [of] from what source I derive those things that are of the highest importance.* |

Notes & Discussion
{13.167–168}

The CONNECTING RELATIVE PRONOUN *quae* (= *et facultas?*) serves to link this sentence to the previous one. The main verb of the APODOSIS, *sentio*, is postponed until the end of the sentence and takes as its object the indirect question (*ex quo... hauriam*). *Illa* is neuter, accusative, plural, and serves as the direct object of *hauriam* even though it stands outside its clause and is separated from it by the relative clause (*quae summa sunt*) that modifies it.

———◆———

38 Atque id eo mihi concedendum est magis quod ex his studiis haec quoque crescit oratio et facultas quae, quantacumque est in me, numquam amicorum periculis defuit.

id concedendum est
    mihi
    magis
      eo

    quod oratio crescit et facultas
        haec quoque   quae periculis defuit
            ex studiis   amicorum numquam
             his   quantacumque est
                                in me

———◆———

39 Quae si cui levior videtur, illa quidem certe quae summa sunt ex quo fonte hauriam sentio.

PROTASIS:

Quae si levior videtur
           cui

APODOSIS:

illa ex quo fonte hauriam sentio
  quae summa sunt

———◆———

| 40 | *For unless by the precepts of many men and by much [study of] literature I had persuaded* |

myself from boyhood that there is nothing in life greatly to be sought if not praise and honor; moreover, that in pursuit of which all tortures of the body, all dangers of death and exile ought to be considered of little importance, never would I have thrown myself on behalf of your safety into such great and so many struggles, and into these daily attacks of depraved men.

Notes & Discussion
{14.168–175}

One of the longer, more philosophical sentences of the oration, the PROTASIS of this past contrary-to-fact condition begins with four separate adverbial words or phrases that postpone until final position the verb *suasissem*, which governs two accusative + infinitive clauses, both with gerundives. In the first infinitive clause, Cicero expands *nihil*, the subject of *esse expetendum*, with the phrase *nisi laudem atque honestatem*, to balance the compound subject of the second clause: *omnis cruciatus...omnia pericula*. In the main clause of the APODOSIS, the direct object (*me*) and verb (*obiecissem*) are separated by a HYPERBATON of some fourteen words that constitute a TRICOLON of prepositional phrases.

40 Nam nisi multorum praeceptis multisque litteris mihi ab adulescentia suasissem nihil esse in vita magno opere expetendum nisi laudem atque honestatem, in ea autem persequenda omnis cruciatus corporis, omnia pericula mortis atque exsili parvi esse ducenda, numquam me pro salute vestra in tot ac tantas dimicationes atque in hos profligatorum hominum cotidianos impetus obiecissem.

PROTASIS:

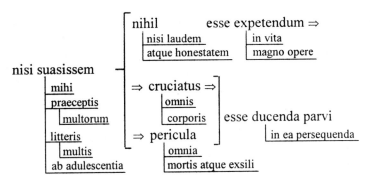

APODOSIS:

| 41 | *How many images of the bravest men, produced [for us] not only for the purpose of studying, but also for the purpose of imitating, have writers both Greek and Latin left behind [for us].* |

NOTES & DISCUSSION
{14.178–180}

The adverb *quam* introduces this exclamatory declaration. *Imagines*, the direct object of the main clause, is separated from its participle, *expressas*, by a HYPERBATON of eleven words. But Cicero is careful to give structure to what intervenes: *non solum...verum etiam* organizes the two gerunds of purpose that are governed by *expressas*, followed by the genitive phrase *fortissimorum virorum*, which modifies *imagines*.

———◆———

| 42 | *And holding these always before me in the administration of the state, I molded my spirit and mind through the very contemplation of [these] excellent men.* |

NOTES & DISCUSSION
{14.180–183}

The framework of this sentence (*ego...animum et mentem ...conformabam*) spans the entire sentence. The CONNECTING RELATIVE PRONOUN *quas* (= *et imagines*) links this sentence with the preceding one, and functions as the direct object of the participle *proponens*, which modifies the pronoun *ego*, emphatically placed immediately following *quas*. Cicero postpones the main verb of the sentence until final position, while its two objects, *animun et mentem*, form the centerpiece, separated from both subject and verb by exactly six words on either side.

———◆———

41 Quam multas nobis imagines non solum ad intuendum verum etiam ad imitandum fortissimorum virorum expressas scriptores et Graeci et Latini reliquerunt!

```
imagines    scriptores   reliquerunt
  multas        et Graeci    nobis
    quam        et Latini

  virorum
    fortissimorum

  expressas
        non solum ad intuendum
        verum etiam ad imitandum
```

———◆———

42 Quas ego mihi semper in administranda re publica proponens animum et mentem meam ipsa cogitatione hominum excellentium conformabam.

```
ego animum et mentem conformabam
                    meam    cogitatione
    quas proponens          ipsa
          mihi              hominum
          semper                excellentium
          in administranda re publica
```

———◆———

| 43 | *These very same illustrious men, whose virtues have been recorded in literature, was it not by means of this particular education, which you extol, that they were educated to greatness?* |

NOTES & DISCUSSION
{15.184–186}

Once again, the main elements of the main clause (*illi...viri...istane doctrina...eruditi fuerunt*) are distributed across the entire sentence, with the subject and verb in first and last position, and two relative clauses bracketing *istane doctrina*, an ablative of means onto which the interrogative enclitic particle *–ne* has been attached.

———◆———

| 44 | *I admit that there have been many men with outstanding minds and virtue, and that they—without [the benefit of] formal education, [but rather] by some nearly divine quality of nature itself—through themselves have stood out as both moderate and distinguished; I even add this: that more often has nature without learning aspired to praise and virtue, than learning without nature.* |

NOTES & DISCUSSION
{15.188–192}

The sentence consists of two independent clauses arranged in ASYNDETON, the first of which contains a compound predicate of two indirect statements connected by *et* and bracketed by the extended HYPERBATON of *ego...fateor*. Both indirect statements contain two ablatives of description (*animo ac virtute :: sine doctrina...habitu*) and end with the PERIODIC placement of their infinitives (*fuisse...exstitisse*) in last position. The verb of the second independent clause, *adiungo*, governs the accusative *illud*, which serves as the antecedent of the indirect statement that follows.

———◆———

43 Illi ipsi summi viri, quorum virtutes litteris proditae sunt, istane doctrina quam tu effers laudibus eruditi fuerunt?

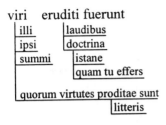

```
viri    eruditi fuerunt
  illi      laudibus
  ipsi      doctrina
  summi     istane
            quam tu effers

  quorum virtutes proditae sunt
                        litteris
```

———◆———

44 Ego multos homines excellenti animo ac virtute fuisse et sine doctrina, naturae ipsius habitu prope divino per se ipsos et moderatos et gravis exstitisse fateor; etiam illud adiungo: saepius ad laudem atque virtutem naturam sine doctrina quam sine natura valuisse doctrinam.

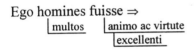

```
Ego homines fuisse ⇒
   multos      animo ac virtute
               excellenti
```

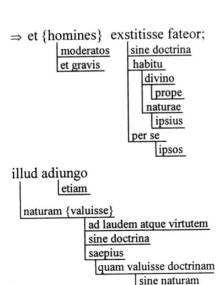

```
⇒ et {homines}  exstitisse fateor;
      moderatos    sine doctrina
      et gravis    habitu
                     divino
                       prope
                     naturae
                       ipsius
                   per se
                       ipsos

illud adiungo
       etiam

  naturam {valuisse}
              ad laudem atque virtutem
              sine doctrina
              saepius
                quam valuisse doctrinam
                  sine naturam
```

———◆———

| 45 | *And I, the self-same person, contend this: that when to an outstanding and illustrious nature* |

has been added a certain method and molding of education, then that certain something, illustrious and remarkable, is accustomed to emerge.

NOTES & DISCUSSION
{15.193–196}

In this brief, straightforward sentence the direct object of the main clause, *hoc*, serves as the antecedent of the accusative + infinitive clause that stands in apposition to it and is introduced by *tum*, which correlates this clause with the *cum ratio…accesserit* clause.

———◆———

| 46 | *And these men, to be sure, if they had not been aided at all by literature in their progress toward* |

achieving and cultivating excellence, would never have applied themselves to the study of these things.

NOTES & DISCUSSION
{16.200–203}

The sentence begins with a CONNECTING RELATIVE PRONOUN that serves as the subject of the PROTASIS and APODOSIS that follow, both of which are PERIODIC in structure: *adiuvarentur* and *contulissent* occupying the final position of their clauses.

———◆———

45 | Atque idem ego hoc contendo: cum ad naturam eximiam et inlustrem accesserit ratio quaedam conformatioque doctrinae, tum illud nescioquid praeclarum ac singulare solere exsistere.

ego hoc contendo:
| idem

      tum illud exsistere solere
         | nescioquid
         | praeclarum ac singulare

      cum ratio confirmatioque accesserit
         | ad naturam
           | eximiam et inlustrem

———◆———

46 | Qui profecto si nihil ad percipiendam colendamque virtutem litteris adiuvarentur, numquam se ad earum studium contulissent.

PROTASIS:

si adiuvarentur
| nihil
| ad percipiendam colendamque virtutem
| litteris

APODOSIS:

Qui...se contulissent
| profecto
| numquam
| ad studium
    | earum

———◆———

47   *Who of us was of so crude and obtuse a mind that*
      he was not moved by the recent death of Roscius,
who, although he died an old man, nevertheless on account
of his excellent skill and charm appeared [as if] he ought
not to have died at all?

Notes & Discussion
{17.214–217}

tam: the adverb, that anticipates the *ut* clause, should be
construed with both *agresti* and *duro*.

————◆————

48   *Therefore that man, only by the movement of his*
      body, had won love for himself from all of us;
shall we neglect the incredible movements of minds and the
nimbleness of talents?

Notes & Discussion
{17.217–220}

The focus of the antithesis between these two independent
clauses is made clear by the pronouns that appear first in their
clauses: in this case, Cicero is focusing on the contrast
between *ille* and *nos*, an antithesis emphasized by the further
parallelism of *corporis motu* in the first clause and
animorum...motus in the second.

————◆————

47 Quis nostrum tam animo agresti ac duro fuit ut Rosci morte nuper non commoveretur? qui cum esset senex mortuus, tamen propter excellentem artem ac venustatem videbatur omnino mori non debuisse.

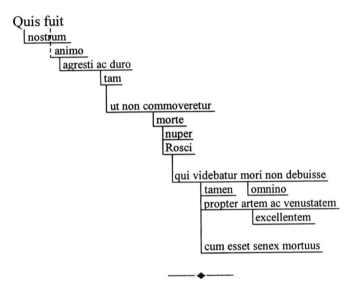

48 Ergo ille corporis motu tantum amorem sibi conciliarat a nobis omnibus; nos animorum incredibilis motus celeritatemque ingeniorum neglegemus?

ille amorem conciliaret;
    tantum   motu
                corporis
             sibi
             a nobis
                omnibus

nos motus   celeritatemque neglegemus
    incredibilis   ingeniorum
    animorum

| 49 | *How often have I seen this Archias, gentlemen of the jury—for I shall use your indulgence, since in* |

this new style of pleading you are listening to me so diligently—how often have I seen this man, although he had written not even a letter, recite on the spur of the moment a great number of the best verses about those things which at that time were going on; how often [have I seen] him, recalled [for an encore] speak the same things with changed words and turns of phrase.

Notes & Discussion
{18.220–226}

The sentence contains two independent clauses, each introduced by the interrogative adverb *quotiens*, and governing an accusative + infinitive indirect statement. Cicero begins with the governing construction of the first main clause (*quotiens hunc Archiam vidi*), but delays the following indirect statement first with the insertion of a parenthetical aside (*utar...attenditis*); then, after repeating the governing construction a second time (*quotiens ego hunc vidi*), Cicero again delays the indirect statement by the insertion of a *cum* clause. Cicero finally allows the direct object of the indirect statement (*magnum numerum optimorum versuum*) to occur, but then delays the verb, *dicere*, with the insertion of a relative *quae* clause. After the completion of the first *quotiens* clause, Cicero introduces a second main clause with the ANAPHORA of another *quotiens*, followed this time only by the accusative + infinitive construction of a second indirect statement, with the governing construction, *ego hunc vidi*, understood from the first *quotiens* clause.

———◆———

49 Quotiens ego hunc Archiam vidi, iudices—utar enim vestra benignitate, quoniam me in hoc novo genere dicendi tam diligenter attenditis—quotiens ego hunc vidi, cum litteram scripsisset nullam, magnum numerum optimorum versuum de eis ipsis rebus quae tum agerentur dicere ex tempore, quotiens revocatum eandem rem dicere commutatis verbis atque sententiis!

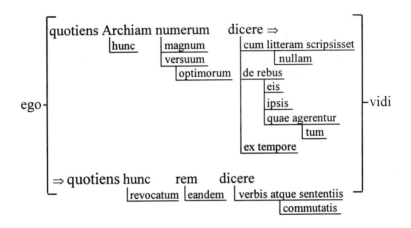

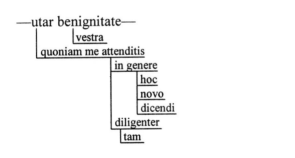

50 *And thus have we learned from the greatest and most learned men: that the studies of other things consist of formal education, instruction, and [technical] skill; [but] that the poet derives his power from nature itself and is excited by means of the power of his imagination, and is inspired as if by some divine spirit.*

NOTES & DISCUSSION
{18.230–234}

The verb of the main clause of the sentence (*accepimus*) governs a bipartite indirect statement, for which the adverb *sic* serves as the antecedent. The two parallel accusative + infinitive clauses, arranged in ASYNDETON, present a comparison between the nature of academic literary pursuits in general (*studia ceterarum*) and the singular nature of the *poeta*. In the first clause of the indirect statement, Cicero employs a single infinitive (*constare*) modified by three ablatives (*doctrina...praeceptis...arte*); in the second, however, he shifts constructions to what is, in effect, the inverse of the first: three infinitives (*valere...excitari...inflari*), each modified by a single ablative (*natura...viribus...spiritu*).

51 *Wherefore, by his own right that Ennius of ours calls poets "holy," because they seem to be recommended to us as if by some gift and grace of the gods.*

NOTES & DISCUSSION
{18.234–236}

This sentence contains a single main clause whose verb (*appellat*) governs two accusatives: a direct object (*poetas*) and an object complement (*sanctos*). The sentence concludes with a *quod* (causal) clause.

quasi deorum aliquo: as its attribution on the diagram shows, this phrase should be construed with both *dono* and *munere*.

50 Atque sic a summis hominibus eruditissimisque accepimus, ceterarum rerum studia ex doctrina et praeceptis et arte constare, poetam natura ipsa valere et mentis viribus excitari et quasi divino quodam spiritu inflari.

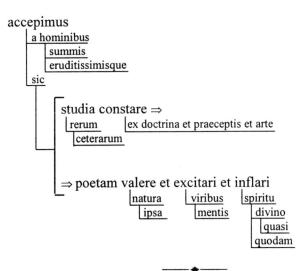

---◆---

51 Quare suo iure noster ille Ennius "sanctos" appellat poetas, quod quasi deorum aliquo dono atque munere commendati nobis esse videantur.

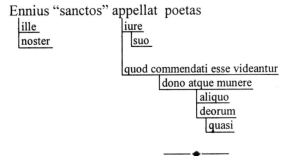

---◆---

———◆———

52 | *Therefore, gentlemen, let this name of poet be sacred among you, most cultivated men, which no barbarity ever violated.*

NOTES & DISCUSSION
{19.237–239}

While the structure of this sentence recalls that of the preceding one (51), the two are not completely parallel. In the main clause Cicero again uses the adjective *sanctum* (the predicate of the independent subjunctive *sit*, it also precedes *nomen* as *sanctos* preceded *poetas* in the previous senence), but the *quod* clause that concludes the sentence is not adverbial but adjectival.

———◆———

53 | *Rocks and deserts respond to his voice; savage beasts are often turned aside by his song and stand still; should not we, also, educated with the best resources, not be moved by the voice of poets?*

NOTES & DISCUSSION
{19.239–241}

The sentence consists of three independent clauses, arranged PARATACTICALLY in ASYNDETON. The first two clauses are statements laying the groundwork for the third, cast in the form of a rhetorical question, hence the shift from the indicative of the first two clauses (*respondent...consistunt*) to the subjunctive (*moveamur*) in the third. Cicero further distinguishes the third clause from the first two with a dramatic shift in subject, which marks the end of the progression from inanimate to animate (*saxa atque solitudines...bestiae :: nos*).

saepe...cantu: construe with both *flectuntur* and *consistunt*.

———◆———

52 Sit igitur, iudices, sanctum apud vos, humanissimos homines, hoc poetae nomen quod nulla umquam barbaria violavit.

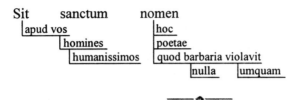

———◆———

53 Saxa atque solitudines voci respondent, bestiae saepe immanes cantu flectuntur atque consistunt; nos instituti rebus optimis non poetarum voce moveamur?

Saxa atque solitudines respondent ⇒
    |voci

⇒ bestiae flectuntur atque consistunt ⇒
    |immanes |saepe
                      |cantu

⇒ nos non moveamur
    |instituti |voce
    |rebus |poetarum
    |optimis

———◆———

| 54 |

Therefore, these men claim [as their own citizen] a stranger because he was a poet, even after [his] death; are we going to reject this man [Archias], while he is living, who is ours both by [his own] will and by [our] laws, especially since Archias for a long time now has devoted all his energy and talent to celebrating the glory and praise of the Roman people?

NOTES & DISCUSSION
{19.246–250}

The structure of this sentence, which contains two independent clauses arranged in ASYNDETON, echoes that of the previous (53): in the first, a statement in the indicative (*expetunt*), sets up the deliberative subjunctive (*repudiamus*) of the second. While Cicero brackets each clause with "bookend" word order of subject and verb (*illi...expetunt* :: *nos...repudiamus*), further emphasizing the antithesis described in each, he deliberately avoids further parallelism within this symmetrical framework: *alienum* in the first clause is not answered by *vivum* in the second, despite the expectation raised by the similar position of both adjectives; instead, Cicero contrasts *alienum* with the relative clause *qui noster est*, and *vivum* with the prepositional phrase *post mortem*. The arrangement is CHIASTIC (*alienum... post mortem :: vivum...qui noster est*).

populi Romani: construe with both *gloriam* and *laudem.*

———◆———

| 55 |

For even as a youth he took up [in his poetry] the Cimbric campaigns, and was on good terms with Gaius Marius himself, who seemed somewhat insensitive to such pursuits.

NOTES & DISCUSSION
{19.250–252}

ad studia: construe with the comparative adjective *durior.*

———◆———

54 Ergo illi alienum, quia poeta fuit, post mortem etiam expetunt; nos hunc vivum qui et voluntate et legibus noster est repudiamus, praesertim cum omne olim studium atque omne ingenium contulerit Archias ad populi Romani gloriam laudemque celebrandam?

illi alienum expetunt ⇒
        quia poeta fuit
        post mortem
         etiam

⇒ nos hunc repudiamus
     vivum
     qui noster est
          et voluntate et legibus

        cum studium...ingenium contulerit Archias
           omne   omne   praesertim
                        olim
                        ad gloriam laudemque celebrandam
                           populi Romani

———◆———

55 Nam et Cimbricas res adulescens attigit et ipsi illi C. Mario qui durior ad haec studia videbatur iucundus fuit.

res [*Archias*] attigit et iucundus fuit
       adulescens   Mario
  Cimbricas   ipsi
                   illi
                   qui durior videbatur
                       ad studia
                         haec

———◆———

56 *Nor, indeed, is there anyone so averse to the Muses who would not readily allow an eternal proclamation of his labors to be committed to poetry.*

NOTES & DISCUSSION
{20.252–255}

A simple, straightforward sentence consisting of a general statement folowed by a relative clause of result (*qui...patiatur*) ANTICIPATED by the adverb *tam*.

————◆————

57 *They say that Themistocles, that greatest of men at Athens, when it was inquired of him what act by way of entertainment or whose voice he would most willingly hear, had said: [the voice] of that man by whom his own virtue would best be celebrated.*

NOTES & DISCUSSION
{20.255–258}

Cicero begins with the emphatic placement of the accusative *Themistoclem*, subject of *dixisse*, the verb of the indirect statement governed by *aiunt*, the main verb of the sentence. In turn, *dixisse* governs its own indirect statement, which is postponed by the *cum...quaereretur* clause, the subject of which is the following *quod...audiret* clause, a bipartite indirect question. The indirect statement dependent on *dixisse* follows the *quod* clause, answering the question posed by the second member of the preceding indirect question (*aut cuius vocem libentissime audiret*). But with the exception of *eius*, which answers the interrogative pronoun *cuius*, the entire indirect statement must be supplied entirely from context (i.e., *eius vocem libentissime se audire, a quo...praedicaretur*).

————◆————

56 Neque enim quisquam est tam aversus a Musis qui non mandari versibus aeternum suorum laborum praeconium facile patiatur.

Neque quisquam est aversus
　　　　　　　　│a Musis
　　　　　　　　│tam

　　　　　　　　　│qui non mandari praeconium patiatur
　　　　　　　　　　│versibus │aeternum │facile
　　　　　　　　　　　　　　　│laborum
　　　　　　　　　　　　　　　　│suorum

———◆———

57 Themistoclem illum, summum Athenis virum, dixisse aiunt, cum ex eo quaereretur quod acroama aut cuius vocem libentissime audiret: eius a quo sua virtus optime praedicaretur.

Themistoclem dixisse aiunt: {vocem se audire}

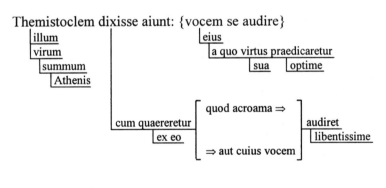

———◆———

58 *Therefore, this self-same Marius likewise especially loved Lucius Plotius, by whose talent he felt those things which he had accomplished could be celebrated.*

NOTES & DISCUSION
{29.258–260}

What begins as a simple sentence with the main clause concludes with a pair of interlocking relative clauses. The first (*cuius...putabat*) governs an accusative + infinitive indirect statement (*ea...posse celebrari*) interrupted by the insertion of a second adjectival relative clause (*quae gesserat*) that modifies its subject (*ea*). While the antecedent of the *cuius* clause is *L. Plotium*, the ablative *ingenio*, on which the genitive *cuius* depends, in turn modifies *celebrari*, the passive complementary infinitive of *posse* in the indirect statement.

———◆———

59 *Indeed, the Mithridatic war, great and difficult and carried out with many vicissitudes on land and on sea, in its entirety by this man was related; and these books illuminate not only Lucius Lucullus, a man most brave and distinguished, but also the name of the Roman people.*

NOTES & DISCUSSION
{21.260–264}

The sentence is composed of two independent clauses joined by the CONNECTING RELATIVE PRONOUN *qui*. The subject of the first clause (*bellum*) is followed by a TRICOLON of adjectives culminating with a participial phrase (*magnum atque difficile et...versatum*). While *totum* agrees with *bellum*, and is therfore attributed to it on the diagram, it is best translated adverbially or as a predicate to *expressum est*. The "bookend" word order of the first clause (*bellum...expressum est*) is repeated in the second (*libri...inlustrant*).

———◆———

58 Itaque ille Marius item eximie L. Plotium dilexit, cuius ingenio putabat ea quae gesserat posse celebrari.

```
Marius L. Plotium dilexit
  |ille                    |item
                           |eximie
              |cuius ingenio putabat ea  posse  celebrari
                                     |quae gesserat
```

———◆———

59 Mithridaticum vero bellum magnum atque difficile et in multa varietate terra marique versatum totum ab hoc expressum est; qui libri non modo L. Lucullum, fortissimum et clarissimum virum, verum etiam populi Romani nomen inlustrant.

```
bellum expressum est;
  |           |ab hoc
  |
  |Mithridaticum
  |magnum atque difficile
  |et versatum
  |totum |
        |in varietate
            |multa
        |terra marique
```

```
qui libri non modo L. Lucullum,  verum etiam nomen inlustrant
                    |virum                   |populi
                |fortissimum et clarissimum  |Romani
```

———◆———

60 *For the Roman people, with Lucius Lucullus commanding, laid open the Pontus, fortified at one time both by royal resources and the very nature of the region; the army of the Roman people, with this same man as leader, with no very great force, routed innumerable troops of Armenians; it is to the credit of the Roman people that the most friendly city of the Cyziceni, by the counsel of the same man, from every royal attack and from the mouth and jaws of the entire war, was snatched and saved.*

NOTES & DISCUSSION
{21.264–271}

A long sentence composed of a TRICOLON of independent clauses arranged in ASYNDETON, each introduced by the emphatic ANAPHORA of a form of the phrase *populus Romanus* and containing a specific reference to Lucullus. Although such repetion raises the expectation of continued congruity between the three clauses, Cicero avoids strict parallelism through variations in language and structure, especially in the third member. In the first two clauses Cicero uses active verbs (*aperuit, fudit*), modifying both with an ablative absolute describing Lucullus' role in the action (*Lucullo imperante... eodem duce*). The third member of the tricolon, however, marks a dramatic shift as Cicero abandons the active voice of the first two clauses for the impersonal construction *laus est*, which governs an accusative + infinitive clause in which the subject (*urbem*) is separated from its two passive infinitives (*ereptam esse atque servatam*) by an extended HYPERBATON of nineteen words.

belli: construe with both *ore* and *faucibus*.

———◆———

60 Populus enim Romanus aperuit Lucullo imperante Pontum et regiis quondam opibus et ipsa natura et regione vallatum, populi Romani exercitus eodem duce non maxima manu innumerabilis Armeniorum copias fudit, populi Romani laus est urbem amicissimam Cyzicenorum eiusdem consilio ex omni impetu regio atque totius belli ore ac faucibus ereptam esse atque servatam.

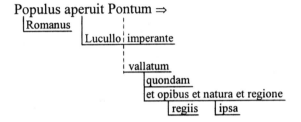

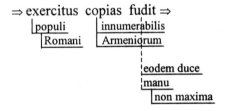

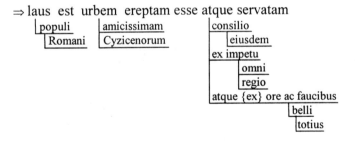

61	*That incredible naval battle off [the island of] Tenedos will always be soken of and proclaimed*

as ours, with Lucius Lucullus fighting, when, with its admirals killed, the fleet of the enemy was destroyed; ours are the trophies, ours the monuments, ours the triumphs.

NOTES & DISCUSSION
{21.271–275}

A series of four independent clauses arranged in ASYNDETON, each introduced by the ANAPHORA of first person plural possessive adjectives, each used predicatively. Yet despite the emphatic repetition of *nostra...nostra...nostra...nostri*, only the last three clauses are parallel. The first clause, which runs to some twenty words, in contrast to the final three, which consist of two words each, completely dominates the sentence. In the first clause, *nostra* is separated from its noun (*pugna*) by a HYPERBATON of eighteen words, within which Cicero inserts two ablative absolutes, one active (*L. Lucullo dimicante*), the other passive (*interfectis ducibus*) and embedded within a temporal *cum* clause. Though weighty, the clause is well-structured, with the two verbs that occur at the beginning of the clause (*feretur et praedicabitur*) balanced by the culmination of the adjectives *incredibilis...illa navalis* which bracket the prepositional phrase *apud Tenedum.*

———◆———

62	*And by whose talents these things are extolled, by these the fame of the Roman people is celebrated.*

NOTES & DISCUSSION
{21.275–276}

The *quorum* clause precedes the main clause, which contains its antecedent (*eis*). And while *quorum* governs the relative clause, and should therefore come first, it instead follows the CONNECTING RELATIVE PRONOUN, *quae* (= *et ea*), which links this sentence to the previous one, and serves as the subject of *efferuntur.*

———◆———

61 Nostra semper feretur et praedicabitur L. Lucullo dimicante, cum interfectis ducibus depressa hostium classis est, incredibilis apud Tenedum pugna illa navalis, nostra sunt tropaea, nostra monumenta, nostri triumphi.

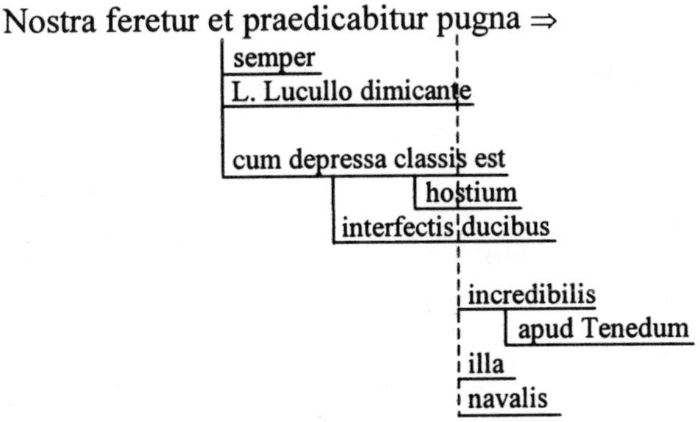

Nostra feretur et praedicabitur pugna ⇒
  semper
  L. Lucullo dimicante

  cum depressa classis est
          hostium
    interfectis ducibus

        incredibilis
            apud Tenedum
        illa
        navalis

⇒ nostra sunt tropaea ⇒

⇒ nostra {sunt} monumenta ⇒

⇒ nostri {sunt} triumphi

———◆———

62 Quae quorum ingeniis efferuntur, ab eis populi Romani fama celebratur.

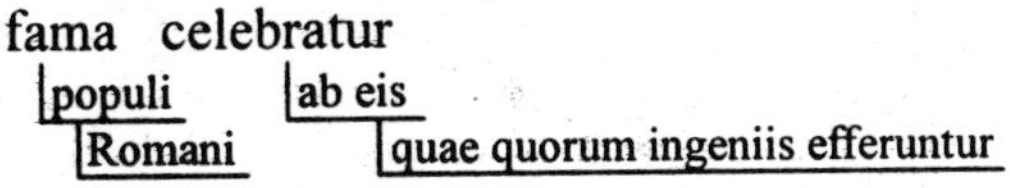

fama celebratur
  populi   ab eis
    Romani   quae quorum ingeniis efferuntur

———◆———

63 *Our own Ennius was dear to the elder Africanus; therefore he is also thought to have been erected in marble in the tomb of the Scipios.*

NOTES & DISCUSSION
{22.277–279}

While the sentence consists of two independent clauses, by introducing the second with the adverb *itaque*, Cicero gives it the force of a result clause loosely anticipated by the adjective *carus*.

putatur: an impersonal passive whose subject is the nominative + infinitive phrase *is esse constitutus*.

————◆————

64 *Therefore, our ancestors received him [Ennius], who had done these things, a man of Rudiae, into their city [as a citizen]; are we to reject this Heraclean man [Archias] from our city, [a man] sought by many cities, but in this [city] established [as a citizen] by law?*

NOTES & DISCUSSION
{22.284–287}

The focus of these two independent clauses, arranged in ASYNDETON, is the ANTITHESIS of "they" (*maiores nostri*) versus "we" (*nos*). Recalling nos. 53 and 54, the first clause states a fact in the indicative (*receperunt*) that gives rise to a rhetorical question with a deliberative subjunctive (*eiciamus*). In the first, direct object, verb, and subject (*illum...maiores nostri...receperunt*) are distributed over the entire clause; in the second, a considerable HYPERBATON separates subject and object (*nos hunc*) from the verb *eiciamus* in final position. In the first clause, adjectival modifiers (*qui...fecerat, Rudinem hominem*) precede adverbial (*in civitatem*); so also in the second, Cicero expands the final two members of an adjectival TRICOLON into participial phrases (*Heracliensem...multis civitatibus expetitum...in hac legibus constitutum*), concluding with an adverbial phrase (*de nostra civitate*) to answer that of the first clause (*in civitate*).

————◆————

63 Carus fuit Africano superiori noster Ennius, itaque etiam in sepulcro Scipionum putatur is esse constitutus ex marmore.

Carus fuit Ennius ⇒
  | Africano | noster
    | superiori

⇒ itaque putatur is esse constitutus
    | etiam | ex marmore
             | in sepulchro
               | Scipionum

———◆———

64 Ergo illum qui haec fecerat, Rudinum hominem, maiores nostri in civitatem receperunt; nos hunc Heracliensem, multis civitatibus expetitum, in hac autem legibus constitutum, de nostra civitate eiciamus?

illum maiores receperunt ⇒
  | | nostri | in civitate
  |
| qui haec fecerat
| hominem
  | Rudinum

⇒ nos hunc   eiciamus
     | Heracliensem | de civitate
                | nostra
     | expetitum
       | civitatibus
         | multis
     | constitutum
       | legibus
       | in {civitate}
         | hac

———◆———

65 *For if anyone thinks that there is less benefit of glory to be obtained from Greek poetry than from Latin, he is seriously mistaken, because of the fact that Greek writings are read in nearly every nation, Latin, however, are contained within their own narrow borders, to be sure.*

NOTES & DISCUSSION
{23.289–291}

As is often the case, the PROTASIS of this present general condition far outweighs the APODOSIS, not only in length, but also in the complexity of its structure. Cicero carefully arranges the elements of the *si* clause in an interlocking order in which the comparative adjective *minorem* anticipates the resolution of *quam*; *putat* anticipates *percipi*, the infinitive of the indirect statement it governs; and the prepositional phrase *ex Graecis versibus* raises the expectation of the corresponding prepositional phrase: *ex Latinis*.

quis minorem… fructum putat ex Graecis versibus percipi quam ex Latinis

Cicero compensates for this imbalance, however, by attaching an adverbial *quod* clause (causal) to the apodosis, which not only explains the denial of *errat*, but also resolves the issue of the difference between Greek and Latin literature raised in the protasis.

———◆———

65 Nam si quis minorem gloriae fructum putat ex Graecis versibus percipi quam ex Latinis, vehementer errat, propterea quod Graeca leguntur in omnibus fere gentibus, Latina suis finibus exiguis sane continentur.

PROTATSIS:

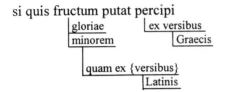

si quis fructum putat percipi
        | gloriae | ex versibus
        | minorem | Graecis

          | quam ex {versibus}
                | Latinis

APODOSIS:

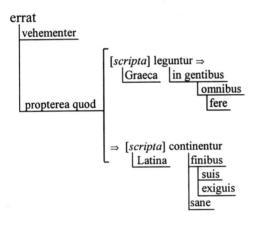

errat
 | vehementer

          | [*scripta*] leguntur ⇒
            | Graeca | in gentibus
                    | omnibus
 | propterea quod | fere

          ⇒ [*scripta*] continentur
            | Latina | finibus
                  | suis
                  | exiguis
               | sane

| 66 | *Wherefore, if those things, which we have achieved, are bound by the regions of the circle of* |

the earth, we ought to desire [our] glory and renown to penetrate to that same place where the weapons of our men have reached; because while not only are these things impressive to those people whose exploits are the subject of writing, but also to those, certainly, who fight for their life for the sake of glory, this is the greatest incentive [for the undertaking] of dangers and labors.

NOTES & DISCUSSION
{23.291-297}

This sentence moves through the PROTASIS and APODOSIS of a simple condition to end with a bipartite *quod* (causal) clause that modifies *debemus*, rather than its two complementary infinitives (*cupere* :: *penetrare*). The two parts of the *quod* clause are set in balance by *cum...tum*.

gloriae causa: because *causa* in the ablative patterns so idiomatically in Latin with a genitive to form a single modifying construction ("for the sake of..."), the entire phrase is diagrammed on a single line.

———◆———

66 | Quare, si res eae quas gessimus orbis terrae regionibus definiuntur, cupere debemus, quo hominum nostrorum tela pervenerint, eodem gloriam famamque penetrare, quod cum ipsis populis de quorum rebus scribitur haec ampla sunt, tum eis certe qui de vita gloriae causa dimicant hoc maximum et periculorum incitamentum est et laborum.

PROTASIS:

si res definiuntur
  eae
  quas gessimus
    regionibus
      orbis
        terrae

APODOSIS:

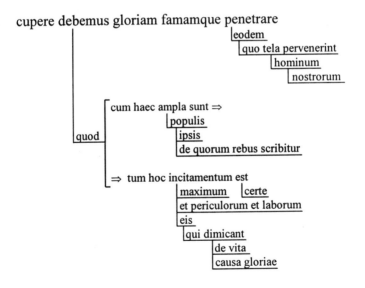

67

Did not our own Magnus [Pompey], who balanced his good luck with his valor, present Theophanes of Mytilene, the writer of his exploits, with citizenship in an assembly of his troops? And those brave men of ours, albeit rustics and soldiers, moved by a certain enticement of glory as if participants of the same praise, did they not aprove this with a great shout?

NOTES & DISCUSSION
{24.304–309}

The sentence contains two independent clauses framed as rhetorical questions introduced by a single *nonne*. Both clauses feature consistent structure, each begining with a series of nominatives (*noster hic Magnus* :: *nostri illi fortes viri*) and concluding with the periodic resolution of the verb in final position (*donavit* :: *approbaverunt*).

quasi participes: although the adjective *participes* agrees with *viri*, together with the adverb *quasi* it forms an adverbial phrase modifying the participle *commoti*, and therefore appears under it on the diagram.

———◆———

67 Noster hic Magnus qui cum virtute fortunam adaequavit, nonne Theophanem Mytilenaeum, scriptorem rerum suarum, in contione militum civitate donavit, et nostri illi fortes viri, sed rustici ac milites, dulcedine quadam gloriae commoti quasi participes eiusdem laudis magno illud clamore approbaverunt?

Magnus Theophanem donavit ⇒

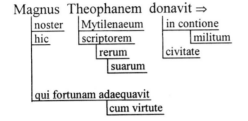

⇒ et viri illud approbaverunt
noster/hic... (diagram)

nostri	clamore
illi	magno
fortes	
sed rustici ac milites	
commoti	
dulcedine	
quadam	
gloriae	
quasi participes	
laudis	
eiusdem	

| 68 |

And we saw in a public assembly that this man [Sulla], when some bad poet from the crowd had presented him with a little book, merely because he had written an epigram about him in some verses of alternating length, immediately from those things which he was at that time selling, ordered a reward to be paid to him—but on this [one] condition: that he not write anything else afterward.

NOTES & DISCUSSION
{25.313–318}

The sentence begins with a CONNECTING RELATIVE PRONOUN (*quem*) that links this sentence with the previous one and serves as the accusative subject of the indirect statement governed by *vidimus*. The placement of *quem* in first position anticipates the infinitive *iubere* which Cicero postpones until nearly the end of the sentence with the insertion of: (1) a *cum* clause; (2) a *quod* (causal) clause; (3) a relative clause modifying *rebus*.

ne quid scriberet: a negative indirect command; while technically an adverbial clause, Cicero is using it here as an APPOSITIVE explaining the ablative *condicione*.

de populo: while prepositional phrases are usually adverbial modifiers in Latin, here the phrase is best construed as modifying the noun *poeta*.

———◆———

68 Quem nos in contione vidimus, cum ei libellum malus poeta de populo subiecisset, quod epigramma in eum fecisset tantum modo alternis versibus longiusculis, statim ex eis rebus, quas tum vendebat, iubere ei praemium tribui — sed ea condicione ne quid postea scriberet.

```
Quem nos vidimus  iubere praemium tribui
         | in contione              | ei
                                    | statim
                                    | ex rebus
                                           | eis
                                           | quas vendebat
                                                    | tum

                                    | sed condicione
                                           | ea
                                           | ne quid scriberet
                                                    | postea

              | cum libellum poeta subiecisset
                             | malus    | ei
                             | de populo

              | quod epigramma fecisset
                                | in eum
                                | tantum modo
                                | versibus
                                       | alternis
                                       | longiusculis
```

69	*Well? From Quintus Metellus Pius, his close associate who presented many with citizenship,*

would he not have obtained [citizenship] either on his own merits or through [the influence of] the Luculli? [Metellus], who especially desired that there be a written account of his achievements to such an extent that even to poets born at Cordova uttering a thick and foreign sound he all the same gave his ears.

NOTES & DISCUSSION
{26.320–325}

familiarissimo suo: although the possessive adjective *suo* agrees with the noun *Metello* and therefore should be diagrammed under it, because the superlative adjective *familiarissimo* is functioning here as a substantive (i.e., as a noun) in APPOSITION to *Metello*, *suo* is best taken as modifying *familiarissimo*, and therefore appears on its own line under it.

———◆———

70	*Nor indeed is this to be hidden, which cannot be concealed, but must be carried out in front of us:*

we are all drawn by a desire for praise, and each best man is led chiefly by glory.

NOTES & DISCUSSION
{26.325–328}

While this sentence contains two independent clauses, because *hoc* in the first clause serves as the antecedent of the entire second clause, the second clause is shown on the diagram under *hoc*.

———◆———

69 Quid? a Q. Metello Pio, familiarissimo suo, qui civitate multos donavit, neque per se neque per Lucullos impetravisset? qui praesertim usque eo de suis rebus scribi cuperet ut etiam Cordubae natis poetis pingue quiddam sonantibus atque peregrinum tamen auris suas dederet.

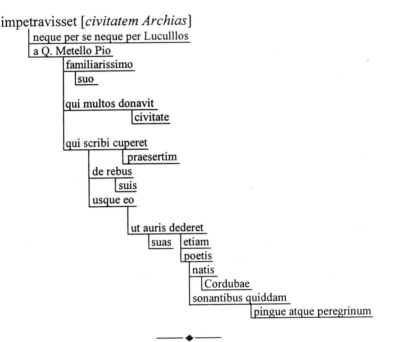

impetravisset [*civitatem Archias*]

70 Neque enim est hoc dissimulandum quod obscurari non potest, sed prae nobis ferendum: trahimur omnes studio laudis, et optimus quisque maxime gloria ducitur.

Neque est hoc dissimulandum, sed ferendum

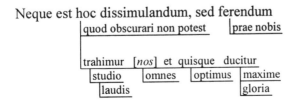

| 71 | *These self-same philosophers, even in those books that they write about despising glory, they inscribe* |

their names; in that very place in which they despise publicity and renown they wish that there be commendation and recommendation for themselves.

NOTES & DISCUSSION
{26.318–322}

The sentence consists of two independent parallel clauses. The subject of both (*ipsi illi philosophi*) is placed emphatically at the head of the sentence, with *in eis libellis quos...scribunt* in the first clause picked up by *in eo ipso in quo...despiciunt* in the second. Both clauses end with the PERIODIC resolution of their main verbs (*inscribunt* :: *praedicari de se ac nominari volunt*).

———◆———

| 72 | *That Fulvius, moreover, who made war against the Aetolians with Ennius as his companion, did* |

not hesitate to consecrate the spoils of Mars to the Muses.

NOTES & DISCUSSION
{27.334–336}

The sentence begins with the demonstrative adjective (*ille*) separated from its noun (*Fulvius*), by a relative clause (*qui...bellavit*). The man verb (*dubitavit*), is in turn separated from its complementary infinitive (*consecrare*) by its direct object (*manubias*) modified by the genitive (*Martis*) and the dative indirect object (*Musis*).

———◆———

71 Ipsi illi philosophi etiam in eis libellis quos de contemnenda gloria scribunt nomen suum inscribunt; in eo ipso in quo praedicationem nobilitatemque despiciunt praedicari de se ac nominari volunt.

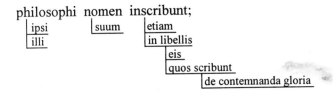

philosophi nomen inscribunt;
  | ipsi | suum | etiam
  | illi | in libellis
                             | eis
                             | quos scribunt
                                         | de contemnanda gloria

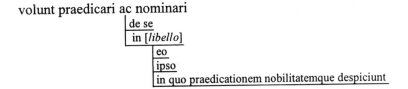

volunt praedicari ac nominari
                       | de se
                       | in [*libello*]
                          | eo
                          | ipso
                          | in quo praedicationem nobilitatemque despiciunt

———◆———

72 Iam vero ille qui cum Aetolis Ennio comite bellavit Fulvius non dubitavit Martis manubias Musis consecrare.

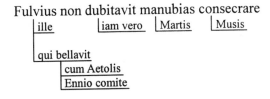

Fulvius non dubitavit manubias consecrare
    | ille | iam vero | Martis | Musis
    |
    | qui bellavit
         | cum Aetolis
         | Ennio comite

———◆———

| 73 | *Wherefore, in which city generals, all but in arms,* |

*Wherefore, in which city generals, all but in arms,
cultivated the name of poets and the shrines of the
Muses, in this [same city] togate judges [i.e., at peace]
ought not to shrink from the honor of the Muses and the
welfare of poets.*

NOTES & DISCUSSION
{27.336–339}

The sentence begins with a subordinate relative clause (*in
qua...coluerunt*) that also contains its anecedent noun (*urbe*),
which should appear in conjunction with the prepositional
phrase that follows (*in ea*), and therefore has been supplied
with it in the diagram.

———◆———

| 74 |

*And, so that you may do this more willingly, I will
now reveal myself to you, gentlemen, and about
my own particular love of glory—a little too keen, perhaps,
but sincere nonetheless—I will confess to you.*

NOTES & DISCUSSION
{28.340–342}

ut id faciatis: because the *ut* clause modifies both *indicabo*
and *confitebor*, it is shown in the diagram on a line that
descends from the *et* that connects the two verbs.

———◆———

73 Quare, in qua urbe imperatores prope armati poetarum nomen et Musarum delubra coluerunt, in ea non debent togati iudices a Musarum honore et a poetarum salute abhorrere.

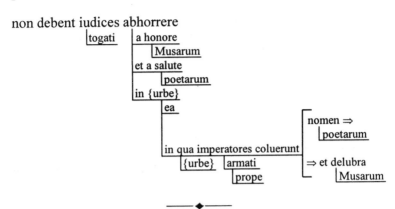

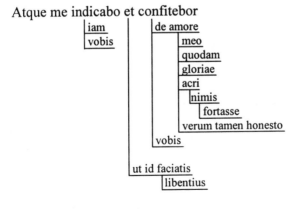

74 Atque ut id libentius faciatis, iam me vobis, iudices, indicabo et de meo quodam amore gloriae nimis acri fortasse, verum tamen honesto vobis confitebor.

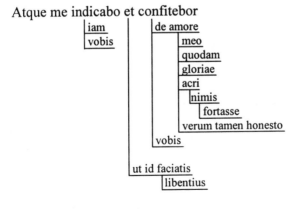

| 75 | *For deeds which we performed in our consulship, together with you, on behalf of the welfare of this* |

city and the entire empire, and on behalf of the life of the citizens and the entire state, this man [Archias] touched on and took up in his poetry.

NOTES & DISCUSSION
{28.342–345}

universa: while the adjective specifically modifies *re*, as does *publica*, the phrase *res publica* is so common in Cicero as to be considered a single term. Therefore, *publica* appears on the diagram together with *re*, and *universa* is shown as modifying both.

———◆———

| 76 | *And to be sure, with this [glory] having been taken away, gentlemen, why is it that we should* |

exert ourselves amidst such labors in this so short and so brief course of life?

NOTES & DISCUSSION
{28.349–351}

The sentence begins with the CONNECTING RELATIVE PRONOUN introducing an ablative absolute (*qua...detracta*). Note the emphatic repetition *tam...tam...tantis*.

———◆———

75 Nam quas res nos in consulatu nostro vobiscum simul pro salute huius urbis atque imperi et pro vita civium proque universa re publica gessimus, attigit hic versibus atque inchoavit.

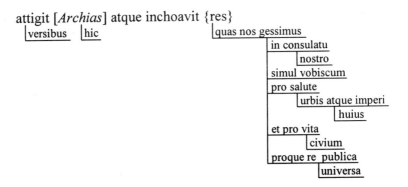

attigit [*Archias*] atque inchoavit {res}
   |versibus |hic |quas nos gessimus
                                          in consulatu
                                            |nostro
                                      simul vobiscum
                                      pro salute
                                          |urbis atque imperi
                                                |huius
                                    et pro vita
                                          |civium
                                    proque re publica
                                          |universa

———◆———

76 Qua quidem detracta, iudices, quid est quod in hoc tam exiguo vitae curriculo et tam brevi tantis nos in laboribus exerceamus?

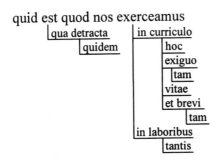

quid est quod nos exerceamus
      |qua detracta |in curriculo
              |quidem |hoc
                           exiguo
                             |tam
                           vitae
                           et brevi
                              |tam
                 |in laboribus
                    |tantis

———◆———

| 77 | *To be sure, if the mind had no presentiment as regards the future, and if, by which regions the* |

span of life is circumscribed, by these same regions it bounded all its thoughts, it would not break itself by such great labors nor would it be tormented by so many cares and vigils, nor would it so often contend for life itself.

NOTES & DISCUSSION
{29.351–356}

This conditional sentence begins with two PROTASES and concludes with a tripartite APODOSIS, rare in Cicero. The second *si* clause is interrupted by the insertion of the *quibus* clause which precedes *isdem*, its antecedent. The three clauses of the apodosis are linked by the ANAPHORA *nec...nec...nec.*

tot: the indeclinable adjective modifies both *curis* and *vigiliis* and so is shown on the diagram on a line between the two nouns.

77 Certe, si nihil animus praesentiret in posterum, et si, quibus regionibus vitae spatium circumscriptum est, isdem omnis cogitationes terminaret suas, nec tantis se laboribus frangeret neque tot curis vigiliisque angeretur nec totiens de ipsa vita dimicaret.

PROTASES:

si nihil animus praesentiret ⇒
     └ in posterum

⇒ et si cogitationes terminaret
    └ omnis └ isdem
    └ suas   └ quibus regionibus spatium circumscriptum est
               └ vitae

APODOSIS:

nec se frangeret neque angeretur nec dimicaret
   └ laboribus └ curis vigiliisque └ totiens
    └ tantis   └ tot   └ de vita
                  └ ipsa

| 78 | *Now a certain virtue resides in each best man, which night and day spurs the mind with the incentives of glory, and reminds it that the memory of our name must not be allowed to slip away with the time of our life, but must be made equal with all posterity.* |

Notes & Discussion
{29.356–360}

The sentence begins with the brief main clause followed by a compound relative clause modifying *virtus* and anticipated by *quaedam*. The second verb of the relative clause, *admonet*, governs two accusative + infinitive clauses.

———◆———

78 | Nunc insidet quaedam in optimo quoque virtus, quae noctes ac dies animum gloriae stimulis concitat atque admonet non cum vitae tempore esse dimittendam commemorationem nominis nostri, sed cum omni posteritate adaequandam.

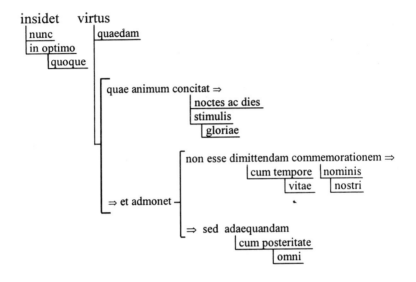

| 79 |

Should we all then, indeed, appear to be of such a narrow mind—who in the state and in these dangers and labors of life are occupied—that, although even up to the last period [of our life] we have drawn no tranquil and peaceful breath, yet still we think that at the same time with us all things will perish?

NOTES & DISCUSSION
{30.360–365}

This sentence poses the first of two rhetorical arguments (for the second see below) introduced by the particle *an.* The framework of this sentence is *tam...videamur esse...ut... arbitremur?* But Cicero delays the *ut* (anticipated by *tam*) with the insertion of a relative clause, and then postpones the resolution of *ut* with the insertion of a *cum* clause.

———◆———

| 80 |

Or [what about] statues and images, representations not of minds but of bodies [that] many of the best men have carefully left behind?—ought we not to prefer all the more to leave behind a representation of our character and intelligence, carved and polished by most outstanding talents?

NOTES & DISCUSSION
{30.365–369}

This compound sentence continues the alternative question begun above. While the particle *an* that introduces the first independent clause serves to link this sentence to the previous one, Cicero inserts *nonne* into the second independent clause to help combine the two clauses into a single unit. Cicero also employs an interlocking word order (genitive plural :: *relinquerunt* :: genitive plural :: *relinquere*) to enhance the overall rhetorical effect:

non animorum...sed corporum...relinquerunt; consiliorum relinquere
    |_____|_____|_____|_____|

———◆———

79 An vero tam parvi animi videamur esse omnes qui in re publica atque in his vitae periculis laboribusque versamur ut, cum usque ad extremum spatium nullum tranquillum atque otiosum spiritum duxerimus, nobiscum simul moritura omnia arbitremur?

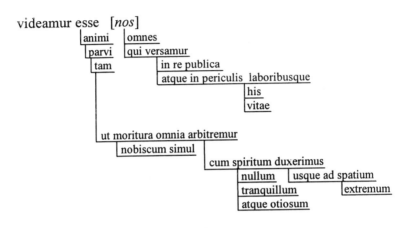

———◆———

80 An statuas et imagines, non animorum simulacra, sed corporum, studiose multi summi homines reliquerunt, consiliorum relinquere ac virtutum nostrarum effigiem nonne multo malle debemus summis ingeniis expressam et politam?

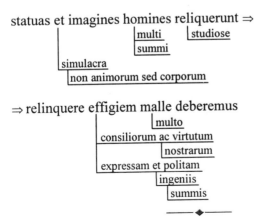

———◆———

| 81 | *I, for my part, thought that all the things which I was doing, even at the very moment I was doing* |

them, I was scattering and disseminating to the eternal memory of the circle of the earth.

Notes & Discussion
{30.369–371}

Ego...arbitrabar: note how the subject and verb of the main clause bracket the accusative + infinitive indirect statement. Note also how Cicero modifies *omnia*, the direct object of both infinitives, with the relative clause *quae gerebam*, playing on the phrase *in gerendo*.

————◆————

| 82 | *Whether this [remembrance], indeed, will be absent from my perception after death, or, as the* |

wisest men have thought, it will [still] pertain to some part of my soul, now at any rate I am certainly delighted by the hope and expectation, such as it is.

Notes & Discussion
{30.371–375}

With this conditional sentence Cicero concludes the CONFIRMATIO of the speech. Both clauses of the compound PROTASIS share parallel PERIODIC structure set in formal balance by the repetition of the *sive* (+ prepositional phrase + verb) construction.

————◆————

81 | Ego vero omnia quae gerebam iam tum in gerendo spargere me ac disseminare arbitrabar in orbis terrae memoriam sempiternam.

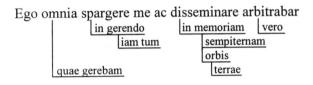

Ego omnia spargere me ac disseminare arbitrabar
in gerendo		in memoriam	vero
iam tum		sempiternam
		orbis
quae gerebam | | terrae |

---◆---

82 | Haec vero sive a meo sensu post mortem afutura est, sive, ut sapientissimi homines putaverunt, ad aliquam animi mei partem pertinebit, nunc quidem certe cogitatione quadam speque delector.

PROTASES:

haec sive afutura est
| a sensu
| meo
| post mortem

sive pertinebit
| ad partem
| aliquam
| animi
| mei

| ut homines putaverunt
| sapientissimi

APODOSIS:

delector
| nunc
| quidem
| certe
| cogitatione...speque
| quadam

---◆---

| 83 | *Wherefore, gentlemen of the jury, preserve a man with a sense of decency that you see is confirmed* |

by both the stature of his friends, as well as by the duration [of their friendship]; [a man] with as much natural talent, moreover, as it is appropriate for that [quality] to be valued, which you see is sought by the judgments of the most important men; [a man] with a case of the kind which is sanctioned by the support of the law, the authority of a municipality, the evidence of Lucullus, and the public records of Metellus.

NOTES & DISCUSSION
{31.376–382}

The first sentence of the brief PERORATIO is long but relatively simple in construction. Cicero begins by introducing the main verb and its object up front, the emphatic position lending greater force to the imperative mood of the verb (*conservate*). Then follows a TRICOLON of ablative modifiers (*pudore* :: *ingenio* :: *causa*), each of which is in turn modified by a dependent clause anticipated by a demonstrative pronoun in the first and third (*eo* ⇒ *quem* :: *eius*(*modi*) ⇒ *quae*), and by the correlative construction (*tanto* ⇒ *quanto*) in the second.

pudore eo quem :: ingenio…tanto quantum :: causa…eius modi quae

83 Quare conservate, iudices, hominem pudore eo quem amicorum videtis comprobari cum dignitate, tum etiam vetustate, ingenio autem tanto quantum id convenit existimari, quod summorum hominum iudiciis expetitum esse videatis, causa vero eius modi quae beneficio legis, auctoritate municipi, testimonio Luculli, tabulis Metelli comprobetur.

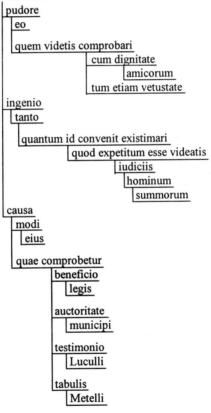

conservate hominem
- pudore
  - eo
- quem videtis comprobari
  - cum dignitate
    - amicorum
  - tum etiam vetustate
- ingenio
  - tanto
    - quantum id convenit existimari
      - quod expetitum esse videatis
        - iudiciis
          - hominum
            - summorum
- causa
  - modi
    - eius
  - quae comprobetur
    - beneficio
      - legis
    - auctoritate
      - municipi
    - testimonio
      - Luculli
    - tabulis
      - Metelli

84

And since these things are so, we seek from you, gentlemen of the jury, if there ought to be not only any human—but even divine—commendation in the presence of such great talents, that this man—who [always adorned] you; who [always adorned] your leaders; who always adorned the accomplishments of the Roman people; who, even during these recent domestic dangers of ours and yours, promises that he will pledge himself as an eternal testimonial of praise; and who is among that number [of poets] who have always been thought to be and therefore proclaimed as sacred in the eyes of all—you should accept into your confidence in such a way that he seems to be relieved by your kindness, rather than injured by your severity.

NOTES & DISCUSSION
{31.382–391}

ut eum accipiatis: although technically an indirect command, the *ut* clause is rendered in the diagram as the object of *petimus*, and so apears on the same line as the main clause. Contained within this *ut* clause is the particle *sic*, which triggers an *ut* clause of result. *Eum*, the direct object of *accipiatis*, is modified by a TRICOLON of relative clauses, the first of which Cicero expands to allow *ornavit* to govern three direct objects; the second governs an accusative + infinitive indirect statement; the third governs is own subordinate relative clause modifying *numero* and anticipated by the pronoun *eo*.

———◆———

84 Quae cum ita sint, petimus a vobis, iudices, si qua non modo humana verum etiam divina in tantis ingeniis commendatio debet esse, ut eum qui vos, qui vestros imperatores, qui populi Romani res gestas semper ornavit, qui etiam his recentibus nostris vestrisque domesticis periculis aeternum se testimonium laudis daturum esse profitetur, quique est ex eo numero qui semper apud omnis sancti sunt habiti itque dicti, sic in vestram accipiatis fidem ut humanitate vestra levatus potius quam acerbitate violatus esse videatur.

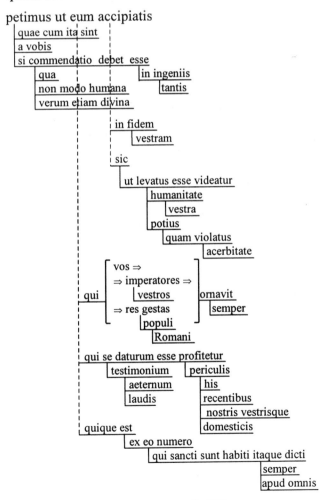

85 *And which things concerning this case according to my custom, briefly and simply, I have stated, gentlemen of the jury—these things I am confident have been approved by all; and which things, alien to the forum and judicial custom, both concerning the natural talent of the man, and, generally, about his craft, I have spoken— these things, gentlemen, by you I hope have been accepted in good part; [that they have been] by that man, who is conducting the trial, I know for certain.*

NOTES & DISCUSSION
{32.392–397}

The final sentence of the oration contains three independent clauses joined by ASYNDETON. The first two clauses are rhetorically linked through parallel PERIODIC construction and the double ANAPHORA of the relative pronoun *quae,* both of which introduce a relative clause, and both of which find their antecedents in the repeated pronoun *ea,* which in turn function as the subjects of two passive indirect statements:

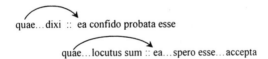

quae…dixi :: ea confido probata esse

quae…locutus sum :: ea…spero esse…accepta

Likewise, in the third and final clause *ea esse accepta* must be understood as the accusative + infintive indirect statement of the main verb *scio.*

85 | Quae de causa pro mea consuetudine breviter simpliciterque dixi, iudices, ea confido probata esse omnibus; quae a foro aliena iudicialique consuetudine et de hominis ingenio et communiter de ipso studio locutus sum, ea, iudices, a vobis spero esse in bonam partem accepta, ab eo qui iudicium exercet, certo scio.

ea confido probata esse;
└quae dixi └omnibus
      └de causa
      └pro consuetudine
            └mea
      └breviter simpliciterque

ea spero esse accepta ⇒
            └a vobis
            └in partem
                  └bonam
└quae locutus sum
   └aliena
   └a foro.┆.consuetudine
         ┆ └iudicali
         ┆et de ingenio
         ┆   └hominis
         ┆et de studio
         ┆   └ipso
         ┆communiter

⇒ scio {ea esse accepta}
   └certo   └ab eo
                  └qui iudicium exercet

APPENDIX

———————◆———————

A BRIEF GLOSSARY
OF TERMS

ALLITERATION — The device of beginning several consecutive, or parallel, words or phrases with the same letter or sound. (EXAMPLE: *Martis manubias Musis* [336].)

ANAPHORA — The repetition of a single word (with the same or different inflection) introducing a series of parallel clauses or phrases, thereby linking them as consecutive units. (EXAMPLE: ***nostra*** *sunt tropaea,* ***nostra*** *monumenta,* ***nostri*** *triumphi* [274–275].)

ANTICIPATION [ANTICIPATES, ETC.] — The use of certain words or phrases (pronouns, adverbs, etc.) to raise the audience's expectation of particular grammatical constructions, dependent clauses, etc. (EXAMPLE: *ab* ***eis*** ⇒ *artibus* ⇐ ***quibus*** *aetas puerilis ad humanitatem informari solet* [42–44]; *hominem pudore* ***eo*** ⇔ ***quem***...*videtis* [376–377].)

ANTITHESIS — The juxtaposition of contrasting terms or grammatical units for rhetorical effect. (EXAMPLE: *cum esset cum M. Lucullo* ***in Siciliam profectus*** *et cum* ***ex ea provincia*** *cum eodem Lucullo* ***decederet*** [77–79].)

APPOSITION — A noun used to describe another noun, usually standing next to it and set off by commas, is said to be "in apposition." (EXAMPLE: *apud praetorem populi Romani, lectissimum virum* [24–25].)

APODOSIS [SEE ALSO BIPARTITE CONSTRUCTION] — The conclusion, or main clause, of a conditional sentence; it usually follows the PROTASIS, but can precede it for emphasis.

ASYNDETON [ASYNDETICALLY, IN ASYNDETON, ETC.] — The arrangement of two or more words, phrases, or clauses, without conjunctions or connectors (e.g., *et*, *atque*, *sed*, etc.), but typically punctuated by editors with a comma or semicolon. For example, a TRICOLON of clauses in ASYNDETON would be arranged one after the other in sequence, without anything to connect them. (EXAMPLE: *Erat temporibus illis iucundus Q. Metello, audiebatur a M. Aemilio, vivebat cum Q. Catulo...*[69–71].)

BIPARTITE CONSTRUCTION — Simply, any construction consisting of two parts, ranging from words and phrases, to clauses and sentences. When one or more elements of the two members are arranged in parallel construction, Cicero may be using the device to underscore antithesis between them. (EXAMPLE: ***ille corporis*** *motu tantum amorem sibi conciliarat a nobis omnibus;* ***nos animorum*** *incredibilis motus celeritatemque* ***ingeniorum*** *neglegemus?* [218–220].)

BRACKETING [SEE ALSO HYPERBATON] — The insertion of a word or phrase between two elements of a separate grammatical construction that syntactically should stand together. Usually, the two words forming the bracket are modified by the words or phrases enclosed by them, and so the entire construction represents a single idea. (EXAMPLE: ***ratio***⇒ *aliqua ab optimarum artium studiis ac disciplina* ⇐***profecta*** [4–5].)

CHIASMUS [CHIASTIC, ETC.] — The reversal of the order of words or phrases in corresponding pairs (A B :: B A), often used by Cicero to achieve ANTITHESIS. (EXAMPLE: *spatium* (A) *praeteriti temporis* (B) *et pueritiae* (B) *memoriam* (A) [8–9].)

COMPARANDUM — A clause containing the second part, or resolution, of a comparison. (EXAMPLE: *si quis minorem gloriae fructum putat ex Graecis versibus percipi* ***quam ex Latinis*** [288–289].)

CONFIRMATIO — The part of a judicial speech where the orator presents his case.

CONNECTING RELATIVE PRONOUN — A relative pronoun that stands at the beginning of a new sentence and serves to connect it to the one preceding in which its antecedent lies. (EXAMPLE: *Archias...venit Heracleam.* **Quae** [= *et Heraclea*] *cum esset civitas...* [79–80].)

EXORDIUM — The introduction, or opening statement, of a judicial speech designed to win the *benevolentia* (good will) of the *iudices* (jury).

EXPOLITIO — The elaboration of a theme previously introduced (employed by Cicero at 351 ff.).

HENDIADYS — An expression composed of two elements, generally nouns, joined by a conjunction, where the sense strictly demands a single modified noun: "law and order" = "the order of law," or, "rainy days and Mondays," = "rainy Mondays." (EXAMPLE: *in iudiciis periculisque* for *in iudiciorum periculis* [35–36].)

HYPERBATON [SEE ALSO BRACKETING] — (1) The separation of a noun and its modifier, usually in order to BRACKET other words or constructions. (EXAMPLE: **Pontum**⇒ *et regiis quondam opibus et ipsa natura et regione* ⇐ **vallatum** [265–266]); (2) in a broader sense, the suspension of any word syntactically necessary to complete a clause or phrase (see PERIODICITY).

HYPOTAXIS [HYPOTACTIC, ETC.] — The opposite of PARATAXIS, it is the occurrence of often elaborate syntactic subordination (i.e., clauses within clauses) in a single sentence; typically, the resolution of one subordinate clause is interrupted by the insertion of another which must be resolved first. (EXAMPLE: *...tam parvi animi videamur esse omnes, qui in re publica...ut, cum usque ad extremum spatium nullum tranquillum...duxerimus, nobiscum simul moritura omnia arbitremur?* [361–365].)

HYSTERON PROTERON — A reversing of the natural order of ideas, as "to fall and slip" where "to slip and fall" would be the natural sequence of events. (EXAMPLE: *praedicari de se ac nominari volunt* [331–332].)

LITOTES — The affirmation of something by the denial of its opposite: "not a few," "not unlike." (EXAMPLE: *non neglegebantur* [55].)

NARRATIO — The part of a judicial speech where the orator presents the facts of the case, such as they are.

OCCUPATIO — The rhetorical device of anticipating an opponent's objection and then refuting it.

PARALLELISM — In effect the opposite of ANTITHESIS, it involves the symmetrical arrangement of a series of related words, phrases, or clauses. (EXAMPLE: ***proximis censoribus*** *hunc cum clarissimo imperatore L. Lucullo apud exercitum fuisse,* ***superioribus*** [*sc. censoribus*] *cum eodem quaestore fuisse in Asia,* ***primis*** [*sc. censoribus*] *Iulio et Crasso nullam populi partem esse censam* [132–135].)

PARATAXIS [PARATACTIC, ETC.] — The opposite of HYPOTAXIS, it is the arrangement of sentences into syntactically coordinate clauses without subordination. (EXAMPLE: *at haec studia adulescentiam acuunt, senectutem oblectant, secundas res ornant, adversis perfugium ac solacium praebent, delectant domi, non impediunt foris, pernoctant nobiscum, peregrinantur, rusticantur* [207–211].)

PERIODICITY [PERIODIC, A PERIOD, ETC.] — A trademark of Ciceronian rhetorical style, it involves the suspension until final position of a word that is syntactically necessary (e.g., the subject or main verb) to complete the sense of a sentence or clause.

PERORATIO — The last section of a speech, it was the orator's "closing argument," in which he would rally all of the themes raised during the course of the speech in a final appeal to the *iudices* (jury).

PROLEPSIS — The use of a word in the clause preceding the one where it should naturally appear: "See the eagle, how high it flies," for "see how high the eagle flies." (EXAMPLE: *Si quid est in me ingeni, iudices, quod sentio quam sit exiguum* [1–2].)

PROTASIS [PROTASES] — The dependent, or "if" clause, of a conditional sentence that anticipates resolution in the APODOSIS, or main clause.

REFUTATIO — The part of a judicial speech containing a rebuttal, or counter-argument, to the opposition's case.

SYNCOPATION [SYNCOPATED, ETC.] — The omission of a letter or syllable from the middle of a word. (EXAMPLE: *donarunt* = *donaverunt* [57].)

SYNECDOCHE — The use of the name of a part for the whole. (EXAMPLE: *animus ex hoc forensi strepitu reficiatur et aures convicio defessae conquiescant* [145–147].)

TRICOLON — The arrangement, or grouping, of three words, phrases, or clauses, often coupled with ANAPHORA. (EXAMPLE: *hoc concursu hominum litteratissimorum, hac vestra humanitate, hoc denique praetore exercente iudicium* [31–33].)

TRIPARTITE CONSTRUCTION — Simply, any construction consisting of three parts, ranging from words and phrases, to clauses and sentences. One of Cicero's favorite rhetorical devices, it is one of the most readily appreciable stylistic features of his oratory. (EXAMPLE: *hoc concursu hominum litteratissimorum, hac vestra humanitate, hoc denique praetore exercente iudicium* [31–33].)

VARIATIO — Any deviation from verbal or structural expectation for the sake of avoiding predictable symmetry or repetition. (EXAMPLE: *famam ingeni exspectatio hominis, exspectationem ipsius adventus admiratioque superaret* [49–51].)

ZEUGMA — A rhetorical device through which a single verb governs two or more objects in different ways: "he held his breath and the door for his wife." (EXAMPLE: *studium atque auris adhibere posset* [63].)

NOTES

NOTES

NOTES

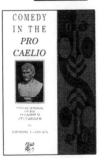

Advanced Placement

Horace: Selected Odes and Satire 1.9
Ronnie Ancona

xxxii + 200 pp. (1999), Paperback, ISBN 0-86516-416-9

Ovid: Amores, Metamorphoses Selections
Charbra Adams Jestin & Phyllis B. Katz

TM: viii + 72 pp. (1999), Paperback, ISBN 0-86516-427-4
Student: xx + 196 pp. (1999), Paperback, ISBN 0-86516-414-2

Vergil's Aeneid, 10 & 12: Pallas & Turnus
Barbara Weiden Boyd

TM: vi + 13 pp. (1998), Paperback, ISBN 0-86516-428-2
Student: xii + 44 pp. (1998), Paperback, ISBN 0-86516-415-0

Vergil's Aeneid, Books I–VI
Clyde Pharr

xvii + 518 pp. (1964, Reprint 1998 with bibliography)
Paperback, ISBN 0-86516-264-6

Cicero's *Pro Caelio,* AP Edition
Steve Ciraolo

xxxii + 192 pp. (1997), Paperback, ISBN 0-86516-264-6

Catullus, AP Edition
Henry V. Bender, Ph.D.
Phyllis Young Forsyth, Ph.D.

TM: 95 pp., 8½ x 11 (1996), ISBN 0-86516-276-X
Student: 105 pp., 8½ x 11 (1996), ISBN 0-86516-275-1

Why Horace? A Collection of Interpretations
William S. Anderson, ed.

xvi + 264 pp. (1998), Paperback, ISBN 0-86516-417-7
xvi + 264 pp. (1998), Hardbound, ISBN 0-86516-434-7

Why Vergil? A Collection of Interpretations
Stephanie Quinn, ed.

(1999), Paperback, ISBN 0-86516-418-5
(1999) Hardbound ISBN 0-86516-435-5

BOLCHAZY-CARDUCCI Publishers, Inc.
http://www.bolchazy.com